WRITING
FOR
IMPACT

WRITING
FOR
IMPACT

8 Secrets from Science That Will
Fire Up Your Readers' Brains

Bill Birchard

HARPERCOLLINS
LEADERSHIP

AN IMPRINT OF HARPERCOLLINS

Published by HarperCollins Leadership,
an imprint of HarperCollins Focus LLC.

Any internet addresses, phone numbers, or company or product information printed in this book are offered as a resource and are not intended in any way to be or to imply an endorsement by HarperCollins Leadership, nor does HarperCollins Leadership vouch for the existence, content, or services of these sites, phone numbers, companies, or products beyond the life of this book.

ISBN 978-1-4002-4149-1 (eBook)
ISBN 978-1-4002-4148-4 (TP)

Library of Congress Control Number: 2023931453

Printed in the United States of America
23 24 25 26 27 LBC 5 4 3 2 1

To the scientists

CONTENTS

PREFACE

I once ran workshops for first-time book authors where I offered eight time-tested strategies for writing better. Those are the eight strategies—or "secrets"—in this book. After coming up with the eight, a question nagged at me: What ties them together? Is there a single principle that explains why they work? What causes readers to keep reading every time you write with one of these strategies?

That question sent me on a journey of scientific discovery. I researched what happens in readers' brains when you use these strategies in nonfiction. What would psychology and neurobiology reveal? What accounts for these strategies' appeal? What mystery magic—*scientific* secret—makes them irresistible in winning over readers?

My initial research pointed to a central finding: When you read, your brain is set abuzz, and much more broadly than scientists once thought. Not just the region known for processing words as symbols starts firing. Many other regions light up, too. This was a revelation to me. I hastily concluded that flashes of neural excitement, by themselves, were enough to keep readers reading.

The central principle of great writing, in other words, was to give readers a full-bodied, full-brain buzz. If you want to please readers, use colorful words, "spark" instead of "cause," "blossom" instead of "develop." Or bursts of metaphor: "feed the mind a tasty treat" lest you "browbeat your readers with boredom." A well-activated brain, like a well-fed stomach, was a well-satisfied one. That was the secret.

I was naïve. Yes, I had worked as a professional writer for more than 30 years. I was on staff at a magazine, worked as a freelancer for several magazines, wrote five books on business, health, and finance, collaborated as a writer on 10 more books, coached other authors in producing yet more books. One book I drafted even became a *New York Times* bestseller. Still, as much nonfiction as I had written, when it came to the science of writing, I was a greenhorn. I was making a newbie's error, grabbing the first convenient idea to explain a complex mystery.

Fortunately, a friend and mentor, John Butman, set me straight. John, a longtime author and premiere book-writing consultant, essentially asked, "Is that all there is to it? The secret to great writing is to spur a pleasurable brain buzz?"

John—whose death in 2020 was such a loss—always looked for deeper meaning. That was his habit and passion: At times a technology writer, he sent me a note saying he wished there were a single "algorithm" discovered by scientists that writers could harness. My brain-buzz-to-pleasure theory was too thin. I had to dig deeper to retrieve the gem of science I needed.

I had been hoping to find this gem without mining a global library of science. But that was not to be. I went back and read hundreds of peer-reviewed scientific papers. I interviewed the leading scientists who wrote those papers. Lo and behold, psychology and neuroscience did reveal the gem I was looking for: Engaging writing not only gives readers' minds a buzz. It spurs their motivational machinery.

Of course, if you've written a lot, you might have sensed as much: To win over readers, you have to motivate them. But science today offers the proof, the evidence of how and why the mind prompts readers to devour your writing—why tempting cues in words have the same motivating effect as tempting cues for food or drink or shelter or sex or a social connection.

The central lesson was simply that you win by playing to those primal, motivating impulses.

If you're a professional writer like me, you may have learned from hard work how to engage readers by motivating them. By putting one word after another, year after year, relentlessly questioning yourself, graciously accepting editors' suggestions, you have gained skills at turning merely informative material into engaging writing. But the science suggests you can avoid some of that hard trial-and-error work. You can let the light of new research guide you.

The good news is that these strategies work for writers of all abilities, so even if you bought this book to be a more effective and influential communicator and do not consider yourself a writer, you will benefit.

As a writer and communicator, you not only need to become a student of the rules of good writing. You need to become a student of human motivation. How to become the model student—a student who knows how to motivate people to start and keep reading—is the purpose of this book. How to become the student, yes, then how to become the master, and then how to write so readers not just get what you're saying but also get engaged. I only wish John were around to see how much he contributed to my new understanding.

REWARD YOUR READER

How do you win over readers with what you write—win them over and whet their appetite for more? Win them over in the same way that the best writers do? You take a tried-and-true approach: You mimic the model that seasoned professional writers offer. Their examples of composition—and their advice—are gold.

That's the rationale you've probably heard in the past—and in school—on how to write with impact: Success comes from learning composition as an art from the masters. An art nurtured by experience, intuition, wide reading, and the experts' examples. An art with rules, of course, but still an art. An art that's subjective.

But recent advances in neuroscience and psychology show that this is only half the story—and often not the most instructive half. Experimental data on people while reading, along with images of their brains, reveal how the human mind reacts to words, turns of phrase, and language of all kinds. Success in writing comes also from learning scientific principles that *prove* the masters' genius. Scientific principles that are objective.

Brain research today shows how evolution shaped our minds as language-processing machines. The initial revelation is that readers, at the level of fundamentals, don't differ much in what they like and what prompts them to respond. The more remarkable one is that you can learn from the evidence which strategies to choose as a writer to best engage readers.

You may already know how to write clearly. Like most people, you have probably learned to string words together to ably argue a point of view. But such basics will get you only so far in the world today. If as a professional you want to break out with influence, if you want to flourish as a communicator, you have to hook readers with something more. You have to *engage* them.

Science shows how to make this happen. If you want to engage readers with description, for example, you compose with specifics. That's one of the most direct routes to create reader engagement. When readers read specific action verbs, their brains get more aroused than with passive verbs. Neuroimaging shows it—in color. The brain's motor circuits fire as neurons reenact a trace of carrying out that action in real life.

Readers respond to specifics fast, too, in tenths of a second.[1] In one experiment, scientists found that specific verbs like "hit," "box," or "strangle" lit up readers' motor neurons more than "fight," a general word of the same kind. "Touch" triggered some arousal, but "pinch" and "tickle" prompted more. "Perform" had kick, but "juggle" beat it.

You may be writing an article, essay, book, white paper, or email. You may cover subjects light or serious, everyday or evergreen. You may be a lawyer or doctor or engineer or professional in business, government, or civil service. You may write nonfiction *and* fiction. No matter. If you want—need—readers to get hooked on what you're saying, science can show you how.

Hundreds of fascinating experiments tell the story. And this story has never before been told because the scientists—psychologists, cognitive scientists, neuroscientists, and others—haven't aimed to serve writers. They haven't sought out a forum to reach the millions of people who must communicate for a living. They have had a different agenda. They have aimed to simply understand the brain. Just how do those 86 billion[2] neurons make sense of the world?

But by interpreting the scientists' work from a writer's perspective, you can learn that engaging writing comes not just from writing with specifics. That's just a start. It comes from writing with emotion. With surprise. With simplicity. With anticipation. With insight. With social cues. And with story.

The scientists' experiments, highlighting the effects of each of these strategies, show what works and why. They provide a road map to transforming the way you communicate. They give you a fresh opportunity: using the insights of science to turn yourself from an able writer to an engaging one.

THE SECRETS

One principle proven by science underlies your ability to make this transformation: Readers hunger for words and phrases and sentences in the same way they hunger for food, friends, family, and sex. They process words just as they do other stimuli in a stream of inputs with beneficial potential.

Their brains then assess them for value—or what scientists call "reward."

The brain is choosy. It wants to know: Is this stimulus worthy? Is the meaning conveyed by these words something I want to pursue? Does that meaning appear to be something I might like? Can I learn and thrive with it?

The "reward circuit," as scientists call it, performs this assessment. (See figure 1.) When readers assess your words as worthy, the circuit makes sure the readers experience desire. This desire comes from a release of dopamine, a neurotransmitter. As the dopamine triggers the desire, it also feeds readers' hunger for more of the same stimulus. The reward circuit, in a sense, serves as a neural-stimulus traffic director. It guides people in satisfying themselves by assessing and consuming worthy things—ceaselessly.

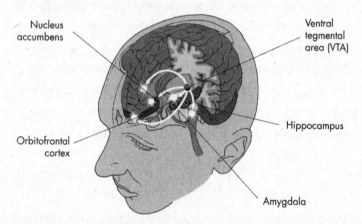

Figure 1: The Reward Circuit. Acting as your brain's motivation engine, the reward circuit releases dopamine when it detects a stimulus worth pursuing. The dopamine creates desire and intensifies your pursuit. If the stimulus—great writing or a great pastry—proves worthy, the dopamine prompts the release of natural opioids. The opioids spark pleasure in five reward-circuit hotspots.

Satisfying the reward circuit is how you engage readers. Doing so in a skillful way allows you to jump from being an ordinary writer to one who stands out from the crowd. It's how great writers stand out—have always stood out—and that's how, in your own profession, you can stand out, too. Winning as a writer is all about playing to the brain's hard-wired and hard-driving reward-circuit desires.

When dopamine gets released in the reader's brain, it carries more than a signal that prompts desire. It also signals that other, more pleasing, chemicals may be in the offing, in particular opioids and marijuana-like substances produced naturally in the brain, including enkephalin and anandamide. The opioids turn on what scientists call reward-circuit "hotspots." When the dopamine, and in turn opioids, work on these half dozen pinkie-size pieces of tissue, readers experience pleasure.[3]

The reward circuit serves as the brain's motivation engine. Its job is to stay forever on the lookout for stimuli people might desire and find pleasure in. If it detects one, it tempts you with a release of that pleasing dopamine-opioid cocktail. That motivates you to keep pursuing the stimulus. If one drink at the cup was good, the reward circuit gives you the impulsive sense that another will be, too.

Your success as a writer in engaging people boils down to satisfying that motivation machine. It's that straightforward. It's that primal. When you choose stimuli with the right hard-wired appeal, you choose to engage readers. Science attests to eight time-tested strategies that help you make that happen. By invoking any or all of them, each long championed by great writers, you play to specific primal impulses. The strategies, eight imperatives, call on you to keep your writing—

Simple

Specific

Surprising

Stirring

And then—

Seductive

Smart

Social

Story-driven

Used alone, each of these strategies drives dopamine-triggered desire. Together, they can win over and hold on to readers you might otherwise lose, because they tempt, feed, and satisfy this basic set of eight primal hungers. So basic are these hungers that you can motivate not just readers with them but people you're communicating with by any means.

Those old rules you learned about communication from school and the masters—embrace them, for sure. You can still win by following writing principles you learned by rote. You can still wow your friends by mimicking the masters. But if you understand how those principles act on readers' minds from scientific experiments, you'll put yourself on the fast track to making decision after decision to communicate with confidence you've never before achieved.

You'll understand not just what strategy to pursue but when and why. And for many people this is a boon. If you have a practical bent—you're analytical and logic-driven—

you'll be drawn to this approach naturally. For too long, you've probably felt as though you had to accept the rules of writing as articles of faith. No evidence showed they worked. Now you have scientific proof. Now when you sit down to write, you can weigh the advice of experts as well as the data.

Which ironically explains why, if you have a creative bent—instinct and feeling-driven—you may also be drawn to this new, revolutionary approach. For too long, you have faced every writing decision as if it were based on artistry—on how the writing "sounds." Success has depended on tapping the intuitive, however much or little you had of it. Now you can rely on scientific evidence as well. This frees up your energy for more artistry when your work demands it.

Whatever your bent, the eight strategies allow you to wield complementary approaches, the subjective and objective. By merging the lessons from experience and the lessons from data, you double your writing skill set. At every juncture, you'll be able to ask not just what sounds right but what's the best strategy (or strategies) based on the science.

You'll always come back to a single keystone principle: Engaging writing is reward-filled writing. You'll ask yourself, What evidence should I use to decide what the best turn of phrase is to reward readers?

The science in this book does not provide a way to learn the mechanics of writing—how to order your thoughts, outline your logic, write complete sentences, and so on. Nor does it give you a microwave-easy recipe to implement the strategies. The eight strategies still demand human, not robotic, judgment. "You can't crank out great writing like sausage meat," as a friend recently reminded me.[4] But the strategies do provide a whole new framework to make sound decisions.

THE ANATOMY OF COMPREHENSION

To grasp the rest of this book, you'll want to know about the anatomy of comprehension. What elements of the brain's structure should you picture in your mind to practice this new framework? You should think of the reader's brain as performing two feats at once. The first is processing meaning. The second is processing reward. The two in fact work interactively. But by taking them one at a time you'll grasp them more easily.

To start, each writing strategy you choose activates different parts of the brain. When you choose a strategy, you are in effect making a decision on which part of your reader's brain to get firing. If you think of yourself as a composer, you're choosing an instrument to start playing. The piece of music you create in the readers' mind is the result of how adept you are at writing music for that instrument.

I'll admit that this can be misleading. Many parts of the brain play together no matter which of the eight strategies you pursue. So I'm simplifying, giving you an easy-to-remember picture. I'm highlighting for each strategy a single—or "signature"—part of the brain that activates. Figure 2 shows this bare-bones representation of the anatomy of comprehension.

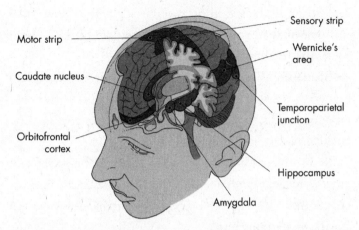

Figure 2: The Brain's Language Processors. After the back of the brain decodes letters, other parts on both sides process words and meaning. Although no writing strategy activates just one brain region—many regions collaborate—one keystone region often gets a starring role. This allows us to isolate a "signature" region for each of the eight strategies.

Simple. When you write with simplicity, you fire up your reader's *Wernicke's area,* a patch of gray matter behind the left ear. The Wernicke's area and other foundational language-processing regions run along the left temple. Although rarely a solo player even for the keep-it-simple strategy, the Wernicke's area acts like a cerebral dictionary, calling up word definitions.

Specific. When you write with concrete or active language, you cue your reader's *sensory and motor strips.* The strips comprise two bands of cortex straddling the top of the brain. The neurons in the strips reenact, or simulate, meaning related to the senses and motor action.

Surprising. When you write the unexpected, you cue your reader's *hippocampus,* which checks what you've written against the reader's memories of facts, places, and events. A seahorse-shaped component in the middle of the brain, it forces the reader to ask, "Is this stuff new?"[5]

Stirring. When you write with emotion, you cue the reader's *amygdala,* which processes the implicit or explicit emotion in your writing. The amygdala acts even before other language areas finish their jobs.

Seductive. When you write to trigger anticipation, you cue the reader's *caudate nucleus.* The caudate fires when you get people to look ahead to anything desirable—words, ideas, stories, or anything else.

Smart. When you write to provoke insight, you cue the reader's *anterior temporal lobe.* This lobe, a patch of the cortex above the right ear (not shown in figure 2), is the telltale zone of action when your reader goes, "Aha!"

Social. When you write to appeal to people's social desires, you cue their *temporoparietal junction,* or TPJ. Readers rely on the TPJ to infer what other people in your writing (including you, the author) are thinking and planning. It's a patch of the cortex on both sides at the rear of your head.

Story-driven. When you write with story technique, you cue your reader's *default mode network,* or DMN. Although the DMN is an always-on network—even if you're on a sofa staring at the ceiling—you excite it especially when your readers sense the start of a narrative. It comprises a half dozen brain parts (the TPJ among them).

So now you have a holistic view of the reading brain. When as a writer you engage readers by using specifics, you fire the sensory and motor strips. When you engage them by using surprise, you fire up the hippocampus. When you engage them by using emotion, you fire up the amygdala. When you engage them by pressing social buttons, you fire up the TPJ. And so on. As a start, you can see just how extensively you activate the human mind when you stimulate it with language.

THE EVOLUTIONARY REWARD

As language processing kicks in, so does the reward circuit. The anatomy of the two overlap. The reward circuit, however, includes unique components like the ventral tegmental area (VTA) and nucleus accumbens. Overall, the circuit comprises a dozen parts largely centered in the middle of your head. The exception is part of the prefrontal cortex (the orbitofrontal cortex, or OFC), which sits just over your eyes. (For simplicity, only some of the principal parts are shown in figure 1.)

As for how the reward circuit operates moment to moment, you can think of its components as working like a panel of experts.[6] Each component, as if caffeinated by dopamine, shares its opinions with the others. Is this stimulus worthy? After a few hundred milliseconds (or less) of kibitzing, they decide on whether to pursue the stimulus or let it go. If the stimulus is a piece of reading, the components ask, "Is this language motivating? Shall I keep on with it?"

When readers process writing they find engaging, they experience desire and, depending on how much it engages them, maybe even an opioid-driven rush of pleasure. That can produce subtle, occasionally striking sensations like goose bumps or shivers down the spine. Even specifics alone can trigger tingles. But you're more likely to turn readers on with several or more primal cues introduced by several or more strategies.

Evolution favored the development of the reward circuit. As humans, to persist on the planet, we needed a system to get ourselves off the beach and make ourselves fit. If we didn't have one, we would have disappeared, victims of sloth, hunger, and weakness. The advent of the reward circuit was thus in some ways inevitable. And once its function was laid down, it operated for thousands of generations to make us continuously stronger and smarter.

Originally, scientists believed the circuit sensed and responded only to basic sensory rewards like food, drink, and sex, says Kent Berridge, a pioneering University of Michigan psychologist and neuroscientist who has studied the circuit for decades. "But it has become clear in the last 50 years from neuroimaging studies that all kinds of social and cultural rewards can also activate this same system"—rewards like art and reading.[7]

Berridge and colleagues including Morten Kringelbach at Aarhus University in Denmark call the pleasure incentive from the reward circuit "evolution's boldest trick."[8] It's that trick, that incentive for action, that lures people day in and day out into doing just about anything. When it comes to writing, if you're going to motivate readers, you need to tap this evolutionary trick.[9]

Readers may then feel it not just faintly but viscerally. Becoming hooked on the reward cocktail is not a figment of their imagination. It's a figment of the attraction created by the flow of neurotransmitters. That attraction can be irresistible—as in when you're reading a page-turner of a novel, or if you're more practical, something as simple and specific as directions to get the most out of the latest app.

The dopamine in the cocktail is not, as formerly thought, a pleasure inducer. Along with spiking desire, it also acts more like a signaling chemical. The dopamine comes from two areas, one featured in the figure, the ventral tegmental area (VTA). (The other is the substantia nigra.) The dopamine flows along multiple key pathways sketched out in figure 1. It thereby wakes us to opportunity and presses us to act. Other neurotransmitters also play a role, but dopamine is the stimulant in the energy drink.

Scientists like Berridge have documented the sequence of action in the circuit. When it first gets going, your initial impulse is to *want* (or desire). If what you're wanting is deemed worthy, the circuit makes you *like* it. If you get sated, it assures you *learn* from what you liked. Wanting, liking, and learning—the dopamine driving each one makes the world of humankind go round.

The biggest payoff, of course, is when the dopamine triggers the release of opioids in your hotspots. Those natural opioids, produced in your synapses, give you a feeling of pleasure.[10] Berridge has revealed that the collection of hotspots usually works together. And when the hotspots work as one with an intense dose of opioids, they essentially produce a feeling of bliss.

Of course, the premier virtue in great writing is clarity. Clearly and accurately conveying your message matters more than anything else. But clarity can only do so much. To really engage readers, to prime them motivationally, you have to use an engaging strategy. Your goal is to get that reward-circuit traffic director to cry out: "There is a chance for good times! We may learn something! Pay attention for a juicy reward cocktail!"

Lewis Thomas, a physician, educator, and writer, knew how to do just that. Here's a passage he wrote about an otherwise unengaging topic, ant behavior: "Ants are so much like human beings as to be an embarrassment. They farm fungi, raise aphids as livestock, launch armies into wars, use chemical sprays to alarm and confuse enemies, capture slaves. The families of weaver ants engage in child labor, holding their larvae like shuttles to spin out the thread that sews the leaves together for their fungus gardens. They exchange information ceaselessly. They do everything but watch television."[11]

Thomas could have dished out facts alone. He could have communicated just fine without keeping it surprising, smart, story-driven, and so on. As a reader, you still would have learned plenty. But he would not have been nearly as able to engage you—and surely would have had less impact on his readers.

Now, you may think that you can't engage people the same way. You write different things. You write to different audiences. You have to be more serious. But the primal impulses that make the eight writing strategies appeal to readers apply just as much in routine writing. Say you're drafting a work email, something mundane. You start: "The project team did a great job in terms of cost and time to completion."

What do you think? That's a decent sentence, right? Why not stick with it? But ask yourself: Am I choosing a writing strategy that plays to primal impulses? Do my words engage?

Have I overlooked one or more obvious strategies to win over readers via the reward circuit?

What if, say, you just made a point to keep it specific? What if you introduced nothing more than an active verb and a couple of specific nouns? Try this: "The project team wowed customers with its hustle and thrift."

Nothing radical, but this new version plays to what readers are wired to want (e.g., specifics), enjoy (e.g., action), and learn from (e.g., insight). You've then produced just a small but distinct increase in rewards. That may not seem like much in one sentence. But small improvements in composition just like that are what successful writers make work for them over and over.

And you can do the same. The big thing to remember: We all have brains motivated to keep reading by the same primal impulses. Everyone loves rewards!

AMAZING REALITIES

We live in a golden era when it comes to learning how to write to engage. Scientists have not only run thousands of experiments that provide the evidence we need. They have run them with readers around the world, using fiction and nonfiction. They have also run them using many kinds of texts, from word lists to metaphors to emotionally charged sentences to entire passages from "The Ugly Duckling" and *Harry Potter and the Sorcerer's Stone*.

The scientists' insights come to us thanks to a range of technologies and research designs. At the simplest, researchers have asked people to read passages and then rate their reading pleasure on a scale of 1 to 7. Or asked people to read a poem, and then measure the people's goose bumps at the end of emotionally charged stanzas—"piloerection" being a sign of arousal.[12] These techniques, using data from self-reports and observable physical reactions, provide an entrée to more complex research.

Recent experiments often rely on imaging technology, software, and data science that allow scientists to see into the brain and differentiate the workings of each part. Scientists today can even measure the firing of single neurons—and thousands of neurons, with perhaps millions of synapses, fit into just a dozen square millimeters of brain tissue.[13] The detail thus revealed gives us a vivid, if not definitive, view of the processing and reward traffic stirred up by words.

Functional magnetic resonance imaging (fMRI) plays a lead role in scientists' research today. The fMRI delineates brain firing into pixel-like cubes no bigger than a cubic millimeter. As with a standard MRI, people are slid into a cavity in a room-size machine. As they read, the apparatus's computer software creates images from the machine's brain scans. Now common in university neuroscience labs, the fMRI has given many neuroscientists a kids-in-a-candy-store level of excitement to try all sorts of experiments never before possible.

The fMRI not only shows high-resolution images of brain anatomy. It also shows, better than an ordinary MRI, which neurons fire and in response to which stimuli. It does so by measuring blood flow in brain tissue as readers process language. Oxygen-rich (unmagnetic) blood floods neurons as they fire and replaces deoxygenated (magnetic) blood. The fMRI distinguishes the two, the result of the brain burning glucose, to create its image.

Scientists face a disadvantage with the fMRI. The machine doesn't show firing in real time. Its signal reflects a couple of seconds of delay, and it peaks only after a dozen seconds or so.[14] The scientists can't tell which word in a sentence is responsible for each fMRI signal. To overcome that limitation, they pair it with an older technology, the electroencephalograph, or EEG.

Scientists often attach two dozen or more EEG electrodes to readers' scalps. Each wire, sometimes sprouting from a shower cap affair, retrieves an electric signal. The EEG can thus record real-time neuronal firing in the gray matter just below the skull's surface. Together, the EEG and fMRI provide scientists both an accurate map of neuronal firing and a precise time lock, to the millisecond, on that firing. They can often link the signal to every word.[15]

Three key findings emerge from this technology that apply to all chapters in this book. They also provide a foundation for many conclusions about reading. First, no matter where on the planet you grew up, your brain, when reading, works in the same way as everyone else's. That's just a fact of our common human ancestry. Whether you grew up in the urban jungle of Beijing or the vernal jungle of Belize, you decode words and process meaning in the same regions.

And it doesn't matter what language you speak, which is amazing given the Linguistics Society of America today counts 6,809 languages worldwide. The Bible, which gives us a rough measure of written languages, has been translated into 2,197.[16] In other words, it doesn't matter if you're speaking

English or German or Chinese or Persian. Your brain taps neurons that evolved hundreds of thousands of years ago to do their work in exactly the same way.

A second key finding is that language comprehension happens in the same way and in the same places whether you're reading or listening. It doesn't matter if you're reading on computers, listening to audio, listening to someone live, or listening to words in a video. Although you decode written letters in one place (at the back of the brain) and the spoken word in another (on the side), you process *meaning* in the same places.

Listening and reading seem so different. How could this be? Scientists have wondered the same thing. But the evidence is undeniable. Fatma Deniz and others at the University of California, Berkeley, asked nine people to alternately listen to and read 10 stories from *Moth Radio Hour*. The stories were identical, word for word. As people read or listened, Deniz and her team scanned their brains with an fMRI. They tracked activity voxel by voxel. A voxel is the brain-imaging equivalent, in three dimensions, of a pixel ($2 \times 2 \times 4$ millimeters in this case).

Deniz's team found that the fMRI signal matched, identically, voxel for voxel, for listeners and readers. It didn't matter how the language entered the brain, by ear or eye. The comprehension pattern matched. The team went a step further, too. They modeled voxel patterns for readers and listeners separately. Then they devised models to predict comprehension patterns. The reader model successfully predicted the processing pattern for the listeners. The listener model predicted the pattern for readers.[17]

The third key finding is that understanding how the human mind interprets language is an ongoing enterprise. It's early days for brain research. The good news for writers, though, is that the details scientists are seeking to reveal in the future are unlikely to change the big picture we have today. The principles will stay the same. How we process meaning, how the meaning triggers rewards, the stimuli that give us feelings of pleasure—that's all governed by the wiring (and rewiring) of the billions of neurons and trillions of synapses in the brain from millennia ago.[18]

Our ability to process words and meaning are a product of a cognitive apparatus that has not changed since humans started farming and living in cities. So, to write with impact, you just have to write so readers feel you're playing to that enduring brain. To its innate hungers. To its relentless desire to want, to like, and to learn to thrive—and flourish. If you're a seasoned writer, you may have learned that lesson from mentors, peers, and experience. If not, you can learn it from the scientists who provide the evidence.

That's when you will make readers wake to your words. That's when you will motivate them to absorb your messages. You will win them over by having merged the subjective and objective, a sense for your reader's ancient, intuitive brain and contemporary, fact-finding one. As you practice the eight strategies, built on the wisdom of science and art, a new Golden Rule for writing will guide you on your way: Reward readers as you would yourself.

CHAPTER 1

KEEP IT SIMPLE

For the Love of Readers: Cut to the Quick

You could argue that if you were to campaign for one habit to win over readers, it would have to be simplicity. True, people sometimes rave about complexity. But they're usually talking about wine, not prose. If you want to engage them, write the simplest sentence you know.

That's one way Ernest Hemingway earned his fans. In *A Moveable Feast,* he wrote to remind himself: "All you have to do is write one true sentence. Write the truest sentence you know"—a sentence, he added, without "scrollwork or ornament."[1]

The allure of simplicity is universal: Pablo Picasso, in a classic pen-and-ink sketch, used just eight lines to depict a toreador whirling around a bull. Johannes Brahms chose just four notes to elevate "Hallelujah" to a celestial refrain. Martin Luther King Jr. repeated four words to reshape an era: "I have a dream."

Don't worry that simplicity will dumb down your writing. Great writers have shown for centuries that plain words serve just fine even for cosmic concepts. John Steinbeck wrote of the desert Southwest in *Travels with Charley:* "At night in this waterless air the stars come down just out of reach of your fingers."[2]

Simple words. A moving image. As if to prove the power of simplicity, Princeton University scientist Daniel Oppenheimer gave 71 Stanford University students two written passages. The two said the same thing, one composed of simple words, the other, complex.

The students, oblivious to Oppenheimer's intent, agreed: The authors of the complex prose were less intelligent.[3] The students apparently had what Hemingway called a natural "bullshit detector"—the big words betrayed the authors' BS.

EASY DOES IT

Why do readers take pleasure in simplicity? Why would evolution have made people thirst for economy in language? Scientists have shown that the first reason is the lighter burden of language processing. Their studies confirm: The shorter your sentence, the simpler your words, the cleaner the syntax, the fewer circuits readers have to recruit for processing.[4] People's brains work faster when processing less, whether it's processing words, pictures, objects, or ideas. They in turn love how you ease their mental load, or as scientists say, boost "processing fluency."[5]

This is what you would expect, of course: All else being equal, less work equals more pleasure. Everyone loves it easy![6] Just as we all like comfort food for dinner, we all like familiar and friendly words for processing. Of course, the human mind can handle plenty of complexity without breaking a sweat. There's nothing like the power of a few billion neurons. So why does simplicity matter so much?

"Our minds want to do things with minimum energy," says Piotr Winkielman, professor at the University of California, San Diego, and an expert in the rewarding nature of processing fluency.[7] Computational efficiency, in which neurons code information in the least energy-consuming ways, he says, reduces that energy.

The region known for basic word processing traces a broad racing stripe along the left side of your brain (although scientists have shown that both the left and right sides of the brain process language[8]). At the rear of the stripe is the Wernicke's area, responsible mostly for word definitions. Although scientists don't know all the ins and outs of how the basic language circuit works, they do know that every neuron pressed into action consumes energy in the form of glucose.

Plenty of experiments reflect the consequences of the burden readers endure if you make your writing complex. When you write sentences with clauses nested in the middle, for example, readers need longer to read them. The nested sentences also prompt more comprehension mistakes.[9] The same goes for sentences that put the objects before subjects ("Profits are loved by investors.") instead of subject first ("Investors love profits.").

The scientists have even quantified the processing burden. When you write using complex sentences, all else being equal, you lower peoples' comprehension accuracy by 10 percent. You also slow reading times for each sentence by a tenth of a second.[10] That 0.1 second doesn't matter if you're not asking people to read much. But what about longer works? What about the thousands of extra 0.1 seconds you pile on in a long report, article, or book?

Heed how the pros make simplicity work for them. Here's writer James Clear in his book *Atomic Habits:* "All big things come from small beginnings. The seed of every habit is a single, tiny decision. But as that decision is repeated, a habit sprouts and grows stronger. Roots entrench themselves . . ."[11] Clear makes his message simple by relying on simple language—it's no accident he's a bestselling author.

Or listen to Kurt Vonnegut as he expressed an opinion related to the subject of this book: "Practicing an art, no matter how well or badly, is a way to make your soul grow. . . . Sing in the shower. Dance to the radio. Tell stories. Write a poem to a friend, even a lousy poem. Do it as well as you possibly can. You will get an enormous reward. You will have created something."[12] Vonnegut trimmed his sentences of tinsel and freed them of fussy words.

RATIONAL CHOICES

One reason simplicity pays off in better processing fluency is that, for all the brain's processing horsepower, it does have limits. You don't win by redlining readers' brains. Psychologist George Miller found in the 1950s, for example, that the longest string of numbers people can store in working memory is seven—as in telephone numbers.[13] The longest string of "chunks" of information, per more recent research, has limits as well. The magic limit for chunks of words appears to be four.[14]

So you can easily bog readers down in a cognitive quagmire. Their motivation to keep reading sags—where's the pleasure in slogging forward? You can also push readers, as Oppenheimer did, into questioning your intelligence, and you might be surprised that science explains why: People normally assume the simpler explanation is the better one.[15]

So universal is that finding that it has a name, "Occam's razor," for William of Ockham, a fourteenth-century Franciscan friar. The razor has passed the test of time because it fits most people's intuition: The better theory is the one with fewer assumptions and parts. The razor's appeal is so strong that people across the spectrum of human thought—in science, math, physics, design, medicine, you name it—embrace it as a given, even if unconsciously. People cling to it like an article of faith.

Why did Einstein earn such kudos for $E = MC^2$? Because (at least in part) the equation defined the physics of energy so economically, using two—just two!—variables. Wouldn't it be nice if you could explain every enigma with just two factors?

Andrey Kolmogorov, a Russian mathematician, took William of Ockham's insight one step better. He proved that information coded in simpler patterns yields better predictions, explanations, and decisions.[16] Leaving the math aside, he made this point: Humans learn from experience that simpler explanations—though not always right—*usually* are.

Consciously or not, people learn to go with the odds. We bet on the least cluttered ideas. We are so inclined in this direction that we risk leading ourselves to stupid conclusions. ("The sun orbits the earth.") We fall for demagogues. (Choose your favorite.) We gorge on fake remedies. (Snake oil.) Still, we learn through experience that the "rational" decision, off the cuff, deems the shorter explanation right.[17]

We do this unconsciously, which underlines how we are more rational beings (doing what "makes sense") and less reasoning ones (doing what's logical).

This in turn explains why many writing teachers suggest your writing contain no more than three big ideas. People comprehend more when you offer less. More than three and you've exceeded Einstein! So if you want to reward readers, be selective and not exhaustive. Put your finger on the single pulse, not on a dozen different pressure points. That's how you'll engage readers and break out with more influence.

You've surely seen how this works in action and appreciated the effect yourself. In a speech instructing life insurance agents, Albert E. N. Gray of Prudential Insurance aimed to explain to salespeople how to succeed. After a long search, he claimed, he had found the "common denominator" among the best agents. It couldn't be simpler, according to his data: "the habit of doing things that failures don't like to do."

One denominator. Not three. Not two. Just one. Better than Einstein! He then went on to explain: "The things that failures don't like to do, in general, are too many and too obvious for us to discuss them here . . . but I think they can all be disposed of by saying that they all emanate from one basic dislike peculiar to our type of selling. We don't like to call on people who don't want to see us and talk to them about something they don't want to talk about."

Simple concept. Simple language. A model of how—and an example of why—to keep it simple: Give readers fewer moving objects to keep track of and they will feel less burdened and more rewarded. Give them too many, and you'll clog their minds with traffic. Gray avoided a parking lot of ideas. He kept people focused on a single center line of reasoning. And that explains why his speech, though written in 1940, circulates on the internet to this day.[18]

FLUENT BENEFITS

Hemingway was hardly the only professional writer to push the benefits of simplicity. Mark Twain, in a letter to a friend: "I notice that you use plain, simple language, short words and brief sentences. That is the way to write English—it is the modern way and the best way. Stick to it; don't let fluff and flowers and verbosity creep in. When you catch an adjective, kill it. No, I don't mean utterly, but kill most of them—then the rest will be valuable."[19]

Twain didn't have data to show he was right. Today we do. To gauge the practical benefits of boosting processing fluency, marketing professor Jonah Berger and his colleagues looked into how long readers stuck with news articles. They checked each of 35,000 articles from nine major online publishers (e.g., *The New York Times*). How far would people scroll before quitting to find something else to read? The results couldn't be clearer: The higher (harder) the readability scores, the sooner people stopped. People didn't like long sentences and words.[20]

Public health professor Tsuyoshi Okuhara and colleagues showed that another benefit of simplicity is that it can give people confidence they can succeed in acting on what they're learning. To test this idea, he and his team asked 400 people aged 40 to 69 to read write-ups on how to exercise for better health. Half of the group got existing directions from health authorities. The other half got an easy-to-read edit. The "simple" group—reading shorter words and sentences, among other things—scored higher on what psychologists call self-efficacy, or the feeling you can and will do something.[21]

A third benefit is that simplicity gives people a sense of affinity for you and your subject. Put another way, your readers feel more a part of your social group. Amazingly, yes, your writing can give people a sense of inclusiveness. People will feel more like subject-matter insiders—even if they aren't. Owing just to that *feeling*, they get more engaged in what you're saying.

We know this because four researchers at Ohio State University asked 650 people to read 80-word write-ups about three specialty technologies. The readers had no particular interest in any of the subjects, about self-driving cars, surgical robots, and 3D medical printers. Half of the people read passages with 10 words of science jargon included. ("This system works because of AI integration through motion scaling and tremor reduction. . . .") The other half read a version with common equivalents. ("This system works because of programming that makes the robot's movements more precise and less shaky. . . .")

As you would expect, readers of the jargony text found the writing harder to process. This was the case even when the researchers tried to compensate for lower processing fluency by giving readers the option of getting pop-up explainers upon mousing over the jargon. That's not too surprising, but here's what is: Quizzed afterward, the jargon readers said they had fewer plans to learn more about the subject. They were also less confident in their knowledge and had lower perceptions of themselves as science and technology people.[22]

In not finding the writing accessible, the readers felt excluded. They stood outside an expert community. They were thus *dis*-engaged. You can begin to see how much harm you can do by not keeping your writing simple. If you want to engage readers, you can't just communicate with any word that conveys a fact. You have to communicate with simplicity that improves readability, gives people confidence in themselves, and makes them feel like they're part of the tribe.

Still another benefit of simplicity is financial. Just one of many examples from corporate finance: Byoung-Hyoun Hwang and Hugh Hoikwang Kim, researchers at Cornell and the University of South Carolina, found that the stocks of investment firms they studied traded 0.7 percent higher if their reports were easy to read. Companies with the easiest-to-read reports traded at *more* than their underlying value (0.35 percent more),[23] in other words, above the actual worth of companies held in the investment firm portfolios.

What's so surprising is that the gain has *nothing to do* with the investment managers working to increase business sales or profits of the companies they hold because they don't manage those firms. They only manage their choice of firms. It stems from writing simply enough that investors can perceive—and bid for—the value of their portfolio of choices, each one priced independently in the larger stock market.

For many years, economists believed financial markets operated "efficiently," incorporating all available information. The research suggests otherwise. Markets incorporate all *accessible* information. No wonder that, in 1998, the US Securities and Exchange Commission mandated that companies use "plain English" in reports to investors. The agency even published a 77-page handbook detailing time-tested tips—cut extra words, use active voice, speak with personal pronouns (e.g., you, your, yours), use common words for jargon, craft short sentences, keep subject, verb, and object together, and more.[24]

All great advice. Advice that applies to communicators in every profession, whether in business, science, health, the humanities, or anything else. If you don't reward your readers with simplicity, you depress the value of your work. Hwang and Kim even suggested hard-to-read reports hurt by putting readers in worse moods—"bothered" and "tense."

SIMPLE ADVICE

How should you define simplicity to gain these benefits? If you're going to use this strategy to reward readers, think of writing simply in two ways. The first is by practicing parsimony. That means keeping your writing free of extra parts. Meister Eckhart advised in the thirteenth century, "The soul grows by subtraction, not by addition."[25] Eckhart wasn't talking about prose, but he could have been.

The second is by practicing elegance. That means constructing your prose with parts put together aptly and ingeniously. Engineers praise the elegance of an arch, a doorway, or a flying buttress. Readers praise the elegance of the arc of your words, paragraphs, or story. In a sense, this echoes an old saying in writing: Keep it as simple as your message allows—but no simpler.

Parsimony and elegance. They are what helped Hemingway write a true sentence. What helped Martin Luther King Jr. reshape an era. What can help you transform yourself as a writer and win over your readers.

Remember that readers want to cruise to the end of a sentence without a slowdown or breakdown in comprehension. They want your words to slide through the doors of their minds without scratching the molding. Here are five tactics to make that happen:

Thin the ads. Obviously enough, if in doubt, use shorter words, shorter sentences, and shorter paragraphs. Going long does have its place in, say, scientific journals, but not in general nonfiction. Simpler wording strikes readers as more honest, likeable, intelligent, reliable, and of course, motivating.

Taking a cue from Twain, one time-tested way to go short is to thin adjectives and adverbs—or "thin the ads." Nouns, powered by verbs, give momentum aplenty.

In case you had any doubt, a team led by psychologist Magdalena Formanowicz asked people to rate two corporate marketing pitches with almost identical messages, one expressed with verbs, the other, adjectives. Asked about the difference afterward, people said the one with verbs made them believe the company was more effective. Verbs, concluded the team, evoke a "let's make it happen" feeling.[26]

An example of this in writing comes from Darrell Huff's *How to Lie with Statistics.* Huff, noting how people use statistics to mislead, delivers his message by focusing on processing-friendly verbs: "If you can't prove what you want to prove, demonstrate something else and pretend that they are the same thing. . . . You can't prove that your nostrum cures colds, but you can publish (in large type) a sworn laboratory report that half an ounce of the stuff killed 31,108 germs in a test tube in 11 seconds."[27]

Break it down. Split up beefy thoughts and sentences. As a pro once said, "The period never comes soon enough."

If it helps you sustain momentum during drafting, write long sentences to start. Sometimes you feel on the first go like you need to deploy extra hardware to nail together a sturdy sentence. The verbal reinforcement seems to strengthen writing that otherwise seems weak. But that's all the more reason to streamline afterward.

Authors Roger Fisher, William Ury, and Bruce Patton took the time to break their big idea into small parts in the opening lines to the classic *Getting to Yes*: "Like it or not, you are a negotiator. Negotiation is a fact of life. You discuss a raise with your boss. You try to agree with a stranger on a price for his house. Two lawyers try to settle a lawsuit arising from a car accident." Five sentences, 46 words, 9.2 words per sentence.[28]

Consider a government report on cigarette-butt emissions. Two scientists wrote: "[Previous] studies only measured freshly generated cigarette butts, or part of the unburned cigarette, and didn't examine the influence of environmental factors that could impact the emissions from cigarette butts, such as temperature, relative humidity, water saturation, ultraviolet (UV) radiation and air change rate."[29]

They could have made that report more engaging by breaking up that sentence to speed processing fluency: "[Previous] studies only measured freshly generated cigarette butts or part of the unburned cigarette. They didn't examine the influence of environmental factors affecting butt emissions. Factors include temperature, relative humidity, water saturation, ultraviolet (UV) radiation and air change rate."

Elementary edit, yes. But the new text, three sentences instead of one, moves the writing one small step toward better processing fluency. And it's many small steps like that which make readers more likely to keep reading. After all, the report had lots to say: People toss 5 trillion butts a year worldwide. As many as four butts per every square meter litter some cities. The butts emit eight nasty chemicals. That's interesting information. But interest alone won't get readers to stick with you if you string them along too long.

The same principle applies to elongated thoughts. People's brains thirst for simple models to represent a complex reality. That's how we make sense of the world. So reward readers by constructing the simplest models possible. Why have magazines with cover headlines that start "The Ten Secrets to . . ." always sold so well? They promise an abstract thought taken apart—and given life—piece by piece in a simpler model.

And yes, as editors hope, they make people feel more motivated, more effective, more savvy to your subject—and maybe even make them feel you're more intelligent.

Cut caveats. Every argument has exceptions. Every topic demands context. Still, beware the fig leaves of hedging. Remember Albert E. N. Gray of Prudential Insurance.

Gray's example of focusing readers on just one big idea is echoed in those old jokes. Investor Warren Buffett: "The first rule of investment is: Don't lose [money]. The second rule of investment is don't forget the first rule."[30] Duke Ellington: "There are two rules in life: Number one—Never quit.

Number two—Never forget rule number one."[31] This book: "Rule number one: Always reward your reader. Rule number two: Always reward your reader."

You can't always express your messages in such an absolute way. Not every piece of thinking can be boiled down to one common denominator. Then, too, as you're developing your big idea, you'll want to cite exceptions, recognize nuances, outline limits, acknowledge gray areas. But when you write second and third drafts, scrub your statements of optional caveats.

If you want to see how a pro does it, you can't do better than Virginia Woolf. Besides writing novels, she assailed the vanities of men in her essays: "Women have served all these centuries as looking-glasses possessing the magic and delicious power of reflecting the figure of man at twice its natural size. . . . Take [the looking glass] away and man may die, like the drug fiend deprived of his cocaine."[32]

Woolf liked hyperbole. She was fond of writing, as she called it, "in the white light of truth." But notice how, by not mincing words, her writing rewarded doubly. She was attempting to answer the question, Why are women so much more interesting to men than men are to women? Her answer came deliciously free of caveats, like an arrow sharpened with simplicity flying straight to the heart.

Delete residue. With each new draft, you'll refine, restate, reinforce, and reiterate. That's all a part of getting what you're saying right. And that's primary. But as your sentences evolve, the entrails of your earlier wording remain. Go back and remove them.

A wonderful thing often happens when you edit to remove residue. You find that the more you simplify, the more you *can* simplify. Nouns yield to pronouns, phrases to words, transitions to nothing. When you clear one layer of excess, you see the next one. You may even enjoy the cleanup job, akin to freeing yourself of castoff doodads at a yard sale.

Phrases like "In order to make this happen" become "To get started . . .". "In keeping with the principles above" becomes "So . . .". "You will frequently find that" becomes "Often . . .". "In terms of how this relates to the subject at hand" becomes . . . zilch.

A lot of these phrases stem from "throat clearing," the verbal noise you make early on while warming up to say something worthwhile. We all hem and haw to get started. That blank screen—when we confront it, it's easy to fill with idle mutterings. But defaulting to filler won't reward readers later.

As an illustration of deleting residue, here's the first paragraph of Charles Darwin's *On the Origin of Species*. Darwin wrote in another era, so criticism is unfair. But you'll see my point. My cross-outs go through what (in 150 years of hindsight) were excesses:

> ~~I will here give a brief sketch of the progress of opinion on the Origin of Species.~~ Until recently the great majority of naturalists believed that species were immutable productions, ~~and had been~~ separately created. ~~This view has been ably maintained by many authors.~~ Some ~~few~~ naturalists, on the other hand, have believed that species undergo modification, and ~~that the~~ existing forms of life are ~~the~~ descendants ~~by true generation~~ of pre-existing forms. ~~Passing over allusions to the subject in the classical writers,~~* the first author who ~~in modern times has~~ treated

it [the subject] in a scientific spirit was Buffon. But ~~as his opinions fluctuated greatly at different periods, and~~ as he does not enter on the causes or means of the transformation of species, I need not here enter on details.[33]

The original word count: 131. After cross-outs: 73. If edited for brevity: about 50.[34] You probably compose Darwin-like introductory phrases while drafting. I certainly do. Who can resist warming up the writing muscles? But once you're off and running, shed the warm-up clothes. Go lean.

Obey copyfit. Don't write more than your reader (or publisher) wants. Compress. Add by subtracting. Remember Picasso and Eckhart and Twain! My copyfit (word count) for this chapter was 4,000 words, so here I stop.

CHAPTER 2

KEEP IT SPECIFIC

For the Love of Readers: Feed the Senses

What happens in your brain when you read "trophy" or "beach" or "nose"? In tenths of a second your visual circuits light up. And what happens when you read "doodle" or "poke" or "ladle"? Your motor circuits fire. And what happens when you read "pizza" or "chocolate" or "coffee"? Your taste circuits light up. And that brings us to the second secret of engaging readers: Keep it specific.

An amusing example illustrating the power of specifics comes from Brian Wansink and others at the University of Illinois at Urbana–Champaign. For six weeks, Wansink and his team arranged to replace generic meal-choice labels with more specific ones at the faculty cafeteria. Out went "Red Beans with Rice," "Seafood Filet," and "Zucchini Cookies." In came "Cajun Red Beans with Rice," "Succulent Italian Seafood Filet," and "Grandma's Zucchini Cookies."

The specifics of the wording apparently whetted people's appetites. Sales of the newly labeled items jumped 27 percent. After eating them, the faculty rated the relabeled items as higher quality. They also said they were more likely to buy the same again.[1] This suggests that rephrasing nouns to be more specific woos people into finding the item labels—and the items—more rewarding.

Of course, smart people probably don't always fall for such tricks. But psychologists and neuroscientists are showing that even trivial specifics sway the brain in ways smart people wouldn't expect. That's in part because specifics play across the brain in ways we don't realize. Specific words wake neurons responsible for processing a range of human senses and sensibilities. We know this because scientists have revealed in fMRI scans the telltale glow of multiple brain regions that swing into action.[2]

Indeed, specifics generate a sort of cerebral virtual reality. Professional writers know this intuitively, and their work makes this apparent. David Brooks, a *New York Times* columnist, once depicted the humility of Americans just after World War II. He wrote: "There were no message T-shirts back then, no exclamation points on the typewriter keyboards, no sympathy ribbons for various diseases, no vanity license plates, no bumper stickers with personal or moral declarations."[3]

Brooks could have stuck with making his point with concepts: "People at that time didn't boast as much, air their opinions as strongly, or write with such bravado." That would have conveyed his message clearly. It's a solid sentence, succinct and easy to process. But it doesn't measure up to Brooks's talent for bringing to bear a catalog of specifics, which jazz a lot more—and more varied—brain circuits.

A SIMULATION MACHINE

Scientists call the processing of specifics in multiple areas responsible for senses and motor action "grounded cognition."[4] This means that readers mentally simulate the sensations and movements conveyed by words. They engage, albeit in a shadowy way, the same parts of their brains that process the meaning of the specific sensations and movements in real life. A word as basic as "salt," for example, fires not just language circuits but those for taste.[5]

In other words, the reading brain does more than translate and retrieve meaning from words as symbols. It reenacts hearing, seeing, smelling, and movement. And it does that job in just one or two hundred milliseconds.[6] As a fun illustration, take this lyric from an old cowboy song: "Me and my boss we had a little spat/So I hit him in the face/with my ten-gallon hat."[7]

As you just read those words, at least three simulations launched. Your visual neurons fired—echoing images of cowboys, a spat, a hat, a face. Your motor neurons fired for arm, hand, and finger movement recruited for hitting. Neurons for sensation in the face fired to experience the slap of the hat. And that was probably only a start.

"Effective communication in language," says Arthur Glenberg, psychology professor at Arizona State University and pioneer in demonstrating grounded cognition, "is when the writer is able to induce these [grounded] activities in the reader's brain. That is, you create simulation and that calls on the readers' experiences" with sensory, motor, and other actions from earlier in life.[8]

Grounded cognition can be hard to believe. For decades most scientists *didn't* believe it. They thought people's brains worked like digital dictionaries. The visual regions in the back of the head translated letter symbols and handed off the words to language-processing regions. The language regions, in particular the Wernicke's area discussed in the last chapter, performed machinelike retrieval of word definitions. From that you understood what people were saying.

Scientists do debate how much readers rely on grounded cognition. Says Benjamin Bergen, professor of cognitive science at the University of California, San Diego, and head of the Language and Cognition Lab, "There's good evidence that there are lots of different processes being engaged all the time. Every sentence you give someone is going to activate most of the real estate in their brain." Bergen characterizes comprehension during reading as a "conspiracy" of processes.

Among the processes getting more attention in current research is a form of statistical processing, neural computation similar to that done by artificial intelligence software that enables computers to write essays.[9] Still, says Bergen, "There appears to be an advantage to more concrete language in terms of its excitation of visual and motor systems. To the extent that one of your objectives as a writer is to create imagery—to create vivid notions a person can experience and then hang on to—that's advantageous."

For analytical people especially, profiting from this advantage may not come naturally. When you sit down to write, concepts often bubble up first. That's the result of the way many people's minds work. The specifics of the past morph into the concepts of the present. The old details resist surfacing. It's as if your mind is saying, "Don't make me dive into the past for the particulars! Just let me get to the point!"

But research shows that, although storing concepts may be more efficient for the brain in the long term, the details drive more simulation in the present. Recognizing the reader's appetite for detail is how you win with the keep-it-specific strategy—and aid your success in every other strategy because all the strategies build on it.

For writers, the question is, What words are best to win the most applause in that theatre of mental simulation? You have to choose the most rewarding sights, sounds, movement, and other details to produce a show that hooks the motivation engine in the reader's mind.

For simplicity in understanding where simulation happens, figure 2 (page 9) highlights the sensory and motor "strips" across the top of the brain. Those strips are prime real estate for simulation, but are by far not the only real estate that gets in the action. Regions for vision (at the back of the head), hearing (side), and smell (front) also rank prominently. You can win over readers by setting any of these brain regions on fire.

SET IN CONCRETE

But let's back up a minute. What specifically does "specific" mean? The straightforward answer is "concrete." That's the term cognitive scientists use. Concrete in all parts of speech, nouns and verbs above all. Concrete words in experiments offer an edge over abstract ones for a couple of reasons. The first one is that your brain processes them faster (all else being equal). Scientists in one study found that readers reacted to nouns like "wallet" and "hospital" almost one-tenth of a second faster than to "saga" and "rarity."[10]

And that aids processing fluency, of course. But another advantage is that readers remember concrete words better.[11] If you ask people to repeat back a list of words they just read, a mix of concrete and abstract, they remember more of the concrete ones.[12]

The degree of concreteness counts. Compare "pelican" to "bird." Or "wipe" to "clean." The more specific words of each pair, according to one study, encode in the brain more richly than the general ones.[13] Readers "feel" and "see" the difference.

We can guess that variety also has benefits. Because specific words target specific regions of the brain, they prompt readers to re-experience different perceptions. What better way to transform your writing than to invoke a range of sensory experience.

As potent as the "concreteness effect" is—as scientists call it[14]—you would think you could almost feel the neurons firing during simulation. The effect would be akin to the firing of muscles during a workout at the gym. Once you started exercising the tissue, you could feel the exertion. But no, readers cannot feel the simulation. Still, you can imagine the impact. As simulation kicks in, readers enjoy a cinema-like mental experience.

You might object that specifics often matter just to titillate and gratify. They offer cheap thrills. But research of the most practical kind tells us they can do much more. Consider the work by two business professors, Grant Packard at York University and Jonah Berger at the Wharton School at the

University of Pennsylvania. They found, in research with a big Canadian retailer, that more specific emails sent to customers get a better reception. Customers not only express more satisfaction. They buy more.

The professors analyzed 1,000 email exchanges, electronic text that went back and forth between a customer and customer-service rep. They found that just a small (but distinct) increase in specifics from the customer-service reps prompted customers to spend around $10 more on goods in the next 90 days, boosting average purchases from $32.73 to $42.80—a spike of 30 percent.

Packard and Berger confirmed what customers were hypothesized to believe—the more concrete emails came from reps who listened to their needs and interests. They in turn created composite examples of what works. Two examples: "You will receive your money back shortly" works better than "You will receive your refund shortly." "Those blue jeans are a great choice" works better than "Those pants are a great choice."[15]

Such trivial specifics. Who would have thought they help sell merchandise? But they have just that kind of power to engage and influence. And via plain text in an email, no less. Such an easy way to win over and get your readers to act.

NEURONS ON FIRE

But how can scientists be so sure that simulation takes place across so many circuits in the brain? The scientists' conclusions rest on a host of experiments. Rolf Zwaan and others at Florida State University conducted a classic investigation of the visual region. They asked students to read sentences with an object that was concrete. They then tested how fast the students confirmed whether a picture shown afterward matched the object. The hypothesis was that if the students had relied on their visual circuitry while reading, in turn priming that neural region, they would react faster afterward.

But there was a twist: Zwaan and his team challenged students to respond to pictures that, without warning, showed the object either in the context of the sentence they just read or not. For example: "The ranger saw the eagle in the sky" was sometimes followed by a picture of a flying eagle. Or sometimes by a picture of a nesting eagle. Or just the reverse: "The ranger saw the eagle in its nest" was followed by a nesting eagle . . . or a flying one.

What do you think happened when readers were asked, Was the object you see in the picture mentioned in the sentence? Readers reacted one- to two-tenths of a second faster with a match—nesting eagle to nesting or flying to flying.[16] The quicker answers provided proof that readers must have initially employed visual regions—separate from language ones—to comprehend "eagle" in the sentences. If they hadn't, the reaction times to both the matched and unmatched pictures would have been the same.

Scientists note that the simulation triggered by language, though it happens in the circuits for vision, is not like the intensive, conscious visualization you might practice in sports. Readers can't afford to vividly visualize all specifics while reading—it would overtax the brain. So they simulate a grainy facsimile of the real thing, which takes up a fraction of the brain tissue and energy. That's of course partly why you're not even aware of it.

This kind of simulation operates for all the senses, not just vision.[17] Specifics, to put it simply, outcompete generalities by waking sense-related brain circuitry in every corner of your mind. Even words related to odor—"oregano," "vinegar," and "turpentine"—drive simulation. They turn on your olfactory circuits. Words like "bell" and "piano" do not.[18]

To get a further feel for the intensity of simulation, all you have to do is read specifics-rich excerpts of engaging writing. Try this passage by former Yale professor William Deresiewicz, as he bemoans the downsides of bureaucracy: "Excellence isn't usually what gets you up the greasy pole. What gets you up is a talent for maneuvering. Kissing up to the people above you, kicking down to the people below you . . . picking a powerful mentor and riding his coattails until it's time to stab him in the back."[19]

Ouch! No abstractness there. No dulling of the intensity of simulation. Similarly, J. K. Rowling, speaking at Harvard University: "The first thing I would like to say is 'thank you.' Not only has Harvard given me an extraordinary honor, but the weeks of fear and nausea I have endured at the thought of giving this commencement address have made me lose weight. A win-win situation!"[20]

Specifics mentally reverberate. Images from fMRI scans reveal how much. In one experiment, when people were asked to react to words related to the mouth, hand, and leg— "I bite an apple," "I kick the ball"—the sentences fired brain regions for shutting the jaw and swinging the leg.[21] That contrasted with the processing of abstract words: "Appreciate" and "judge" don't trigger the same flurry of activity.[22]

Subtleties matter, too. A team led by Simon Lacey at Emory University compared people reading literal sentences to those reading sentences with the literal meaning replaced by a common texture-related metaphor. Examples: "Life is a challenging road" versus "Life is a bumpy road." "The logic was vague" versus "The logic was fuzzy." "He has a deceitful personality" versus "He has a slimy personality." The sentences with metaphors, trite as they were, fired up people's sensory regions. The literal ones didn't.[23]

Scientists over the years have often exposed readers to artificial reading conditions—to lists of solo words or truncated phrases. That has prompted others more recently to investigate whether concreteness has the same effect in normal texts. Rutvik Desai and researchers asked people to read selected paragraphs from "The Emperor's New Clothes" by Hans Christian Andersen.[24] Their question: Will people reading text with nouns high in "manipulability"—objects you control with your hands—experience more intense firing in the brain's motor regions than people reading text with nouns low in manipulability?

Let's join the emperor's entourage. Here's a passage as he shows off his "magnificent outfit": "The noblemen who were to carry his train stooped low and reached for the floor as if they were picking up his mantle. Then they pretended to lift and hold it high. They didn't dare admit they had nothing to hold."

If you're like the people Desai and his team cocooned inside an fMRI machine, the concrete, manipulable nouns ("train," "mantle") sparked a bright signal in your brain's planning and skilled-action regions.[25] This contrasts with words in other parts of the story like "mirror" and "fools." As a reader, you're right there trailing the emperor with your hands on his mantle.

MUSCULAR DICTION

The potency of simulation is hard to overstate. One reason is that its impact doesn't stop in the brain. It extends to the body. Michael Spivey and his colleagues at Cornell tracked the eyeballs of people listening to stories that describe movement. They wondered: Would neurons in the mind, once engaged by words denoting movement, excite muscles in the eyes to follow that movement? More generally, would grounded cognition transfer from the brain to muscle fibers?

Here's one of the team's stories: "You are standing across the street from a 40-story apartment building. At the bottom there is a doorman in blue. On the tenth floor, a woman is hanging her laundry out the window. On the twenty-ninth floor, two kids are sitting on the fire escape smoking cigarettes. On the very top floor, two people are screaming."

You can probably guess. People's eyeballs, monitored by a special eye-tracking device, turned up, in the direction of the story flow. What's more, their eyes followed the movement in other stories no matter if the direction suggested was up, down, or sideways. People's eyeballs—and this with eyelids shut—followed the motion in the text.[26]

Which for researchers raised a related question. Might eye movement simulate the speed of movement in stories, too?

Yes, other experiments have shown they do.[27] And what about other body muscles getting excited from different neural simulation? A variety of muscle fibers, as measured by muscular electrical signals, reflect the meaning of action words.[28]

Reactions in the body, in other words, aid understanding in the mind. The nervous system, muscles, and even viscera get involved in the comprehension process.

That your mind and body reprise the real thing makes sense if you think about it. Arizona State's Glenberg notes that your brain learned words at the same time you engaged motor and sensory neurons to explore objects as an infant, toddler, and child. You touched objects, mouthed them, and manipulated them. You learned their names as you got to know them. "Those interactions," he says, "shaped your sensory and motor system used in language understanding."

"Even when you learn math, you learn to count with your fingers," he notes. That explains why experiments with people reading numbers, "nine" for example, drive the motor area linked to finger counting.[29] Says Glenberg, "It doesn't take too much of a leap to see how that education is playing out in adult cognition."[30]

We can guess that William Deresiewicz had people re-enacting a kiss and a kick. Not only their lip and leg motor neurons reacted to his wording. Their facial and leg muscles did as well—and maybe even their guts driven by emotion, as we'll learn in chapter 4. The cooperation of the entire body made comprehension that much more vivid.

You have to wonder: Who's talking to whom at each step in comprehension? Mind to body or body to mind? And how far back, as a wide-eyed infant, did you learn to process language via that mind-body dance step?

So responsive are people to motor detail that you can—literally—put readers in the shoes of the people you write about. As proof, John Stins and a team from the Netherlands, Sweden, and Germany checked to see if action sentences would influence readers' posture. Would the neural activity reflecting effort implied in a text be mirrored in people's stance? Would foot pressure inferred from the text and simulated in the brain be revealed in the sway of their bodies?

Stins's team had readers stand on a "force plate." People read sentences implying no, high, or low effort. Examples: "The nurse admires the patient," "The nurse is lifting the patient," "The nurse is lifting the plant." The plate gauged how much people shifted their stance. Now think about this for a second. Stins's team was asking if words, first, were processed "lexically," that is, by their definition in the Wernicke's area; second, "semantically," via simulation in motor circuits; or third, "somatically," with the help of the body itself.

The readers—who had no idea what was going on—answered that question. They swayed to the side subtly with the high-effort sentences. They didn't do so while reading low or no-effort ones.[31] This was remarkable. Comprehension bounced signals from mind to body, and in fact, readers, completely unaware, did put themselves in someone else's shoes.

So you can see how far you fall short of your potential in rewarding readers if you don't take grounded cognition into account while writing. If you have a great idea for a new

app for airline customers, you could just say that it will save
people time, money, and trouble. But you could instead say
that it will allow them to cut to the front of the line, pad their
airline-mile accounts, and soothe their stress headaches. Your
specifics will get their whole being in the action.

PRIZING SPECIFICS

So as a writing strategy, "keeping it specific" ranks high in its
potential for helping you transform your writing to be more
engaging. You do need to put it in larger context, however.
For one thing, in spite of what I've said so far, concrete words
aren't the only ones that engage readers' sensory and motor
circuits. Abstract ones do, too—just not so directly and often
not as much.[32]

If you write, "He loved his land," readers still simulate what
you mean. That is, they react in more than just the language-
processing parts of the brain. They even do so with words as
intangible as "thought" or "logic."[33] "Frequency," for example,
drives back-of-the brain regions for rhythmic movement.

How this works prompts debate among scientists. But
most researchers agree that grounded cognition of abstract
words, not unlike concrete ones, stems from the circumstances
in which you learned them. "Fitness," for example, may be
abstract, but you learned what it means from exercise. So it
makes sense that the word sparks firing in the neurons for
hand movement. "Beauty," though especially vague, is a word
we learn while observing pretty things. So, no surprise, the
word sparks firing in the visual region, as if you're simulating
viewing pretty pictures.[34]

If you write with abstractions, in other words, you don't lose out on simulation. You still drive action outside readers' symbolic language circuits. If you're a business writer, you could still count on sparking a faint glow of engagement in readers' motor neurons by writing, say, "We need better leadership in management." But you'd spark a lot more if you went further: "We need leaders who walk the factory floor and shake hands with new recruits."

Keeping it specific, like every writing strategy, is also subject to an old principle: Too much of any good thing can become a bad thing. A free-for-all of adjectives, nouns, verbs, and detail makes tedious—not engaging—reading. You have to weigh the pros and cons of each choice of word and phrase. If you don't have a good reason to detail the toppings on your customer's ice-cream dessert, don't. It will create a distraction. You'll communicate less, not more.

Neuroscientist Bergen writes in his book *Louder Than Words,* "It's not your fault if you can't help seeing an elephant when told not to. It's just an automatic part of understanding language."[35] So don't put elephants and other animals in your writing if you don't want them to loom large in readers' minds. Rogue beasts running amok, no matter how irresistible, splinter the reader's focus and reduce, not boost, rewards.

You ultimately face two choices about specifics: One is precision. How specific is enough? If you're writing a tech manual on how to sanitize an R&D lab, do you say "clean" or "wipe" or "sponge" or "scour" or "bleach"? If you're neutralizing an oil spill, do you "pour," "flood," or "sprinkle" the waste oil with chemicals? If you're advising an emperor with no clothes, do you coach, manipulate, or indulge?

As Mark Twain said, "A powerful agent is the right word. Whenever we come upon one of those intensely right words in a book or a newspaper, the resulting effect is physical as well as spiritual, and electrically prompt."[36]

The other choice is quantity. How heavily do you load sentences with detail? When you're adding ice-cream toppings, remember that, paradoxically, per the last chapter, selectivity can have as much or more impact than detail. With that in mind, here are five tactics to harness the science to win over readers with specifics.

Get elemental. To deceive is good, to trick is better, to entrap is best. Choose the most precise meaning with the most specific word. Did you transport new employees or bus greenhorn recruits? Did the first responders struggle in the smoke or wheeze from the toxic fumes? Does the new drug create a feeling of instability or make people's heads swim and the room spin?

George Orwell, like Twain, seemed to anticipate the neuroscience when, in "Politics and the English Language," he wrote, "It is better to put off using words as long as possible and get one's meaning as clear as one can through pictures and sensations. Afterward one can choose—not simply *accept*—the phrases that will best cover the meaning."[37]

Again, you don't have to be writing anything fancy to make this tactic reward readers. Say you're writing advice for insurance adjusters on handling angry customers. You start: "A hotheaded customer barking at you on the phone? Keep in mind that a smiling voice is a happy voice. If you hear gnashing of teeth, speak into the roar with a smile. When you brim with goodwill, you defuse anger. . . ."

Rouse senses, action. Readers want to feel life in your writing. So, evoke the sights, sounds, and motion of the theatre.

In a letter to the shareholders of Amazon, founding CEO Jeff Bezos went the action route. He wrote, "Third-party sellers are kicking our first-party butt. Badly."[38] He could have written, "We're facing strong competition from third-party sellers." But the motor verb scored more simulation points—and we can guess, released that dopamine-driven chemical cocktail among investors.

Even if your subject is unmoving or inanimate, your writing need not be. Say you're an architect. You're describing the effect of installing new cafeteria windows. You could write to clients, "People will be able to look out on that beautiful bank of spruce trees." You could also write: "When people throw open the shades, they'll watch that row of spruces marching toward the horizon, piercing the sky."

In *The Souls of Black Folk*, W. E. B. Dubois does the same thing in a more somber, inanimate setting: "The evening sunbeams had set the dust to dancing in the gloomy chapel."[39] The scene is made engaging not just by a static image but by movement. You see the dust in flight as if in the opening of a movie.

Resolve abstraction. Abstractions have their place, but you can ground them to your advantage with concrete words.

Chief Crowfoot of the Blackfoot Nation: "What is life? It is the flash of a firefly in the night. It is the breath of a buffalo in the wintertime. It is the little shadow which runs across the grass and loses itself in the sunset."[40]

"When we know something well," writes Steven Pinker, a cognitive scientist at Harvard, "we don't realize how abstractly we think about it. And we forget that other people, who have lived their own lives, have not gone through our idiosyncratic histories of abstractification."[41]

So like Chief Crowfoot, reverse engineer the finishing of abstractions. What detail was in their construction and framing? Offer people ready-made specifics to build their own simulation. Life, in the hands of Chief Crowfoot, comes off not as abstract. A flash, a breath, a shadow—the details blossom like magic into a reality you can touch, feel, and see.

You can do the same thing with details to resolve abstractions like "marketing" or "justice" or "pain" or even "weather." Author Zane Grey described the arid weather of the U.S. Southwest: "Thin, clear, sweet, dry, the desert air carried a languor, a dreaminess, tidings of far-off things, and an enthralling promise. The fragrance of flowers, the beauty and grace of women, the sweetness of music, the mystery of life—all seemed to float on that promise."[42]

Fashion handles. What shorthand can you give readers to capture your topic? Can you craft a sticky byword, keyword, or phrase?

Authors often make handles the titles of books. Malcolm Gladwell coined "the tipping point." John McPhee, "basin and range." John Gray, "men are from Mars, and women are from Venus." Nassim Nicholas Taleb, "black swan." Sebastian Junger, "the perfect storm." Rachel Carson, "silent spring."

"Silent spring," for example, became a handle for a big idea: Chemicals like DDT destroy both the natural and human environment. Birds in your backyard are going to disappear if humankind doesn't get control of its manufactured chemicals. Plainspoken handle, yes, but it gave readers a ready—and enduring—grip on her message.

What if you took a cue from Carson? How could you apply her "season" formula? You could call a round of layoffs "the pink-slip summer," a discovery of embezzlement "the autumn of corruption," or the crunch of meeting a deadline "the week of working endlessly."

In his book *The Emperor of All Maladies*, Siddhartha Mukherjee adopted the concept of "war" as a handle: "In a sense, this [biography of cancer] is a military history . . . there are victories and losses, campaigns upon campaigns, heroes and hubris, survival and resilience—and inevitably, the wounded, the condemned, the forgotten, the dead."[43]

Run the show! "Show, don't tell." That's one of the oldest dictums in writing. Too many writers, though, don't grasp its potential to engage. Now that you know the science, you could rephrase the advice: "*Run* the show, don't talk about it."

Even if you're the author of government documents, you can stage a performance. "Tuesday, September 11, 2001," starts *The 9/11 Commission Report*, "dawned temperate and nearly cloudless in the eastern United States. Millions of men and women readied themselves for work. Some made their way to the Twin Towers, the signature structures of the World Trade Center. . . . Among the travelers [in airports that day] were Mohamed Atta and Abdul Aziz al Omari."

The 9/11 report was a longtime bestseller, and not just because of its riveting topic. Its authors tapped simulation for impact, re-creating a visual journey—and more. They at least unconsciously knew that when you light up the stage, you light up readers' minds. Writing is a performance art.

One caution: When you run the performance, you may default to highlighting only what people see. This is intuitive. The brain circuits dedicated to vision take up a big chunk of all mental real estate—at least 20 percent, not counting many interrelated neurons. But don't skimp on simulating other perceptions that set other parts of the brain on fire.

Author Marc Reisner, writing about water issues, sensitizes readers to the rigors of the untamed Southwest desert: "To really experience the desert you have to march right into its white bowl of sky and shape-contorting heat with your mind on your canteen as if it were your last gallon of gas and you were being chased by a carload of escaped murderers."[44]

Now that's a performance. Of course, there are still these questions: Which specifics offer the right reward for my readers? Which colorful word makes the right handle? Which bumper sticker tagline will make my report pop? Just how much chocolate should I shave onto my verbal parfait? Science doesn't offer a direct answer. But it does offer a new basis for a decision: What's the likely simulation?

CHAPTER 3

KEEP IT SURPRISING

For the Love of Readers: Delight with the Unexpected

When an acquaintance kisses you on the cheek unexpectedly, what do you feel? Surprise? Perhaps pleasurable surprise? Science shows that at the top of what gives you a stroke of mental pleasure is unexpectedness. It can deliver joy not just when you're reading, but when you're doing just about anything, so long as the surprise is beneficial.

Brain imaging shows as much, and once again evolution explains why: Your mind guesses what's ahead. It's a prediction engine.[1] After seeing what happens, it rates each stimulus for its unexpectedness. If it confirms the prediction, that's fine—but often boring. "Violation" of the prediction, on the other hand, holds promise, because it alerts you to a chance to learn.

That's how people since the beginning of history made themselves better—better able to survive and thrive. They paid attention to surprises as a way to find opportunities to learn to improve themselves. And that's why writing with a keep-it-surprising strategy is the third secret to engaging

readers. People are thirsty to evaluate surprise of every possible kind for value.

Professional writers know from experience they can
communicate with impact this way. As a start, they show it
by writing with surprising observation. John McPhee: "A
sign—'Slow, Children at Play'—has been bent backward by
an automobile."[2]

Or they show it with analogy. Science writer Ed Yong:
"Each of our body parts has its own microbial fauna, just as
the various Galapagos islands have their own special tortoises
and finches."[3]

Or with metaphor. Writer Joan Didion: "Grammar is a
piano I play by ear, since I seem to have been out of school
the year the rules were mentioned."[4]

Or word combination: Curators at the Little Bighorn Battlefield National Monument write that soldiers in the 1870s
referred to their plight as "*glittering misery*."[5]

In experiment after experiment, scientists have shown that
your brain predicts nonstop.[6] When as a writer you upset readers' predictions with something of greater value, you crank their
reward circuits more than readers expected.[7] Driven by a primal
impulse to heed and value novelty and surprises, readers then
become increasingly engaged by your meaning.[8]

THRIVING ON REWARDS

Scientists speculate that our brains react to unpredicted
stimuli for especially practical reasons. A surprise in hunter-
gatherer times was not always a good thing. It could signal
harm on the way. If you wanted to stay healthy in a forest

with flesh-eating animals, you had to prize any stimulus loaded with surprise. A surprise could also signal a way to get an edge over rivals—or how to enjoy the good life with food, friends, mates, and more.

Every time your brain encounters surprise, an odor, picture, word, or anything else, it pings the reward-circuit neurons to, in essence, ask: Is this worth heeding? *Do I want this? Will I like this? Will I learn something from it?* If your reward circuit says yes, you get a surge of motivation to attend to the surprise, sometimes as earnestly as if your well-being depended on it.

By prioritizing stimuli that come as surprises, the reward circuit promotes, as scientists say, "exploratory behavior." It encourages you to expose yourself to new places, social gigs, food, talk, and more. When you're reading, the high value put on surprise encourages you to press on to the next sentence. As the dopamine cocktail takes effect—as it builds anticipation for the expected pleasure—you can't resist sticking around to see what's next in store.[9]

Scientists often use pictures as the stimuli in experiments to show this effect. They ask people to look at, say, nine similar objects or landscape scenes, and without warning, a different one. When they track people's brains with an fMRI, the tenth image gets a neural novelty circuit to light up. This novelty-specific circuit includes a memory champion in the midbrain, the hippocampus, and the key value assessor, the orbitofrontal cortex, just above the eyes.[10]

The orbitofrontal cortex, also a part of the reward circuit, decides if the novelty is worthy. If so, dopamine continues its work to focus your attention and enhance perception. Some scientists call this the "exploration bonus." It's a potent bonus, too, underlining how much evolution favored reinforcing people's inclination to explore. The effect of the dopamine can last up to 10 minutes, keeping your motivation, reward processing, and learning rolling for an extended period.[11]

Neuroscientist Gregory Berns and colleagues took an offbeat approach to investigate the motivating effect of surprise. They wondered how people would react if taken by surprise by a drink. They asked 25 adults to lie in an fMRI machine with a tube in their mouths attached to a computer-controlled syringe pump. At various intervals, the pump shot pleasant bursts of either fruit juice or water onto their tongues.

To create predictable runs, the Berns team alternated squirts of juice and water every 10 seconds. To create unpredictable ones, they pumped out squirts at random. You might think that reward pathways would light up a lot more for fluids people liked best. Or that people's reward pathways would light up just from enjoying any kind of refreshing fluid, since to people holed up in an fMRI, both water and juice were rated as pleasant.

Not so on either count. The Berns team's fMRI images showed that excited neurons, specifically those in the heart of the reward circuit (the nucleus accumbens), liked squirts best when they came unpredictably. Amazingly, the people didn't consciously realize their preference, either. They said they didn't *feel* a pleasure difference from the surprising squirts. But the fMRI scans showed their reward center neurons *did*.[12] The pleasurable effect was subliminal.[13]

SURPRISE BIAS

You may not have thought surprise could affect you so much. Cognitive science professor Jean-Louis Dessalles at Télécom Paris showed just how much people like surprise in language, in particular in stories. He had people read 18 short narratives. Each was truncated just before the ending. He then gave the readers three choices to close each story. The research question was, Which would the readers choose?

Here's one of the narratives: "Two weeks after my car had been stolen, the police informed me that a car that might be mine was for sale on the Internet. They showed me the ad. The phone number had been identified. It was the mobile phone number of . . ." The choices Dessalles offered for the ending: (a) my office colleague; (b) a colleague of my brother's; (c) someone in my neighborhood. Which one would you choose? In 17 of the 18 stories, people scored the most unexpected option, (a), significantly higher.

People are reflexively drawn to what's surprising. This fact aligns with other research, which shows that most of us devote *one-third* of our language time each day to unexpected events. We start doing so in early childhood.[14] The hard wiring is some of the most basic in the mind.

Just how far will people go to pursue surprise? As you might assume, scientists have found that people won't get jazzed for just *anything* new. Our brains filter surprises. You would go crazy if every stimulus, barely perceived, got serious processing. The volume of data from your eyes, ears, nose, mouth, and skin would drown you in mental effort. What's more, you would get a flood of irrelevant information. Who would want an alert every time a fly flits by? Or a dog barks?

The mind does this filtering both consciously and unconsciously. It first wants to know: What's worthy? What's worth wanting, liking, and learning from? Neurotransmitters in the brain, without your even knowing it, don't just promote the good stuff. They suppress the noise and minutiae. They make sure you ignore meaningless surprises and favor stimuli that fit your goals—good or bad, fun or chilling. Only if the reward circuit says "go" on a surprising stimulus's value in meeting your goals does the dopamine do its motivational work.[15]

When it comes to the effect of surprise from language, some scientists theorize that in ancient times humans learned a Goldilocks rule—to prefer "just the right amount" of unexpectedness.[16] Too much was numbing; too little, boring. As with simplicity and specifics, a balance paid off best.

Take as an example this epigram written by nineteenth-century essayist Charles Lamb: "A pun is not bound by the laws which limit nicer wit. It is a pistol let off at the ear; not a feather to tickle the intellect."

What do you think of Lamb's balance of surprise—aside from his view of puns? Not too hot, not too cold, but just right for your brain to eat it up? Whatever your opinion, winning over people with surprise comes from not letting the pistol of surprise sound either too loud or soft.

PREDICTION RULES

Scientists studying surprise have spent a lot of time defining it. Most would agree that, at its most basic, it's something different from what you anticipate. And for writers, that's probably a good enough definition. In experiments, scientists distinguish *unexpectedness* from *novelty*. That's because you can have the first without the second, but not the second without the first. The brain handles the two a bit differently.

But for a writer's purposes, a surprise starts with prediction. The reader's neurons, acting like jumpy preschoolers, field stimulus after stimulus. As they do, they raise their hands and shout out their guesses for what will come next, the word or phrase or idea or even part of speech. If they're right, basing their judgment on previous experience, they sprint over the expected words, which can aid in processing fluency. If the unexpected appears, they instead shout out an alert.

Katherine DeLong and others at the University of California, San Diego, demonstrated just how eagerly people predict. Her team did so by putting together a set of sentences that appeared to lead toward an easily predictable ending with a noun, but they didn't give the noun. An example: "The day was breezy, so the boy went outside to fly . . ." What's your guess of how that sentence ends? Probably "a kite"—and you predicted that finish even before I suggested you think about it.

DeLong and her team added a small manipulation to assess the presence of prediction. After the verb "fly," they inserted one of two possible articles, either an "a" or an "an." That allowed them to distinguish with an EEG the difference in signal between an insertion that dictated a noun you did or did not expect. If you didn't expect it, the faulty expectation would spur surprise. The key signal would come when the

DeLong team's readers were about to encounter a noun that begins with either a consonant or vowel they didn't expect.

The EEG signal was the tipoff. That's because when you complete a prediction with a word, your brain emits a signal about 400 milliseconds later—in the case of the experiment, after "auto-completing" the last, and most probable, word. This "N400" EEG signal marks the moment of full cognition. With that in mind, read the sentence again, and after the verb "fly," insert an "an." If you came at this cold, what would you predict? Although you probably would at first be predicting "kite," when you hit the "an," you would experience surprise and shift to, say, "airplane."

The "an," an unexpected bump in your prediction machine, sends up a stronger EEG signal. The spiking N400 shows your hypersensitivity to words you didn't predict. With that experimental setup, DeLong and her colleagues had people read lots of sentences, 160 of them, with their scalps wired with 26 electrodes. Each sentence cut off before the last noun, some with an expected article ("a" or "an") and some an unexpected one. Over and over, when articles differed from what people expected, the EEG signal spiked at 400 milliseconds.[17]

The experiment confirmed that people are not just reading the words. They're predicting them *before* reading them. They place their bets in advance.[18] What's especially surprising about prediction with words is that it doesn't affect just language-processing and reward regions. It goes as far as engaging the sensory and motor circuits. Remarkably, you get so far ahead of yourself that you not only predict words about to appear but get other parts of your brain to simulate their meaning. Your simulating mind, your grounded cognition, works ahead of your eyes.

Luigi Grisoni and a team at the Freie Universität Berlin took this finding a step further. They asked people to listen to 138 simple action sentences—such as, "I take the broom and I . . . sweep." They repeatedly found that the motor circuits for people's hands ramped up two-to-three-tenths of a second *before* the word "sweep" appeared. The same thing happened with the motor circuits for facial muscles when people read sentences such as, "I take some grapes and I . . . eat."

Even when Grisoni and his team tricked people—giving them the word "smoke" to end the first sentence instead of "sweep," giving them the word "write" instead of "eat" to end the second—people's motor circuits fired for the predicted (not actual) word.[19] As readers, we simulate preemptively. That sets us up for a double surprise—a surprise at the word and a surprise at our faulty simulation.

Maybe that's why punchlines to some riddle-like jokes work. Our brains get a kick at the instant we realize our prediction *and* simulation machines have jumped to off-base conclusions. "What were the last words of the man at the diner?" The punchline: "I'll have the mushroom soup." What prediction were you making and simulating in your mind? Likely the last words and actions of the man before he paid and left. The brain's prediction machine set you up for folly—and fun—when you realized you had it all wrong.

GUESSING GAINS

Your reading brain is doing an awful lot of work before, during, and after each word. All the neuronal firing, from prediction, simulation, and comprehension, boggles the mind. Only by having billions of neurons can you read anything of more than a few words and get all the processing done. But what about the processing in the reward circuit? How does that figure in? What happens when you surprise people, for example, but the surprise is humdrum? Does that get the reward circuit going, too?

Judith Gerten and Sascha Topolinksi at the University of Cologne asked that question in a stripped-down form. They had people read strings of nine randomly chosen letters and then, after people got used to the pattern, followed with a surprise symbol. The experiment, using trivial stimuli on purpose, aimed to separate surprise from other factors that might influence the reward circuit. They learned what you would expect: When asked to rank each string on a one-to-ten scale, people did reliably rank the out-of-pattern strings as surprising—but they didn't feel any liking (and often disliking).[20]

So yes, even boring surprises gain attention. But they won't create engagement. If you want to win over readers, reject sham surprises. Just as cheap surprises on April Fools' Day fall flat—remember the time you hid your partner's car keys?—so do cheap surprises in writing. An arcane word pulled from the thesaurus won't help your cause. Neither will surprising specifics that go off message. Gimmicks don't reward. You need a feather with value to tickle the intellect.

If you're going to use the keep-it-surprising strategy, what measurable benefit will it have? One piece of evidence comes from Jonah Berger and Katherine Milkman at the University of Pennsylvania. In their study of 7,000 articles from *The New York Times*, they found those rated as surprising by independent judges got on the "most emailed" list 14 percent more often. (An example: "Passion for Food Adjusts to Fit Passion for Running," about a restaurateur who ran marathons.)[21]

In another study, Ahmed Al-Rawi at Concordia University found the same thing. He looked at seventeen elements of the "most retweeted" stories in four newspapers (*The Wall Street Journal, The New York Times, The Guardian,* and *The Washington Post*): The element judged by independent coders that most commonly drove virality of stories in 195,000 tweets? "Unexpectedness/odd/surprising" content. That was the top-ranked item 15.3 percent of the time. ("Social significance" was second, "awe," third.)[22] Surprise, it appears, tugs on readers' reward-circuit neurons like the string on a kite.

Scientists find that surprise benefits readers in other ways. "Atypical" wording, in one study, was shown to get readers to read faster, as it signaled to readers that they were about to learn something new.[23] Other studies show that, when people encounter something novel, they encode it better in memory.[24] Remarkably, they also better encode incidentals that happen right before and after the novel item. This "spill-over" effect occurs even if the incidentals are *not* novel.[25]

The memory advantage comes with a caveat, though. In what's called the "verbatim effect," readers don't recall precise wording very well. They remember meaning better. If you're one of those people who can't repeat a joke or anecdote with all those original delectable turns of phrase, you're normal. That's because, for efficiency's sake, your brain turns strings of words into shorter concepts for storage. Ironically, as much as it likes the novelty, it may easily let go of it in memory.[26]

SURPRISE TACTICS

Surprise can, and should, serve as an always-on strategy when you communicate. It amps up other writing strategies to engage readers doubly.[27] You can surprise with simplicity. Surprise with specificity. Surprise with smarts. And so on. Sweetened by surprise, every writing strategy becomes that magic feather to tickle your readers' brains. Here are five tactics for harnessing surprise to engage your readers.

Prize novelty. Can you pluck uncommon specifics to express common ideas? Can you cook up novel turns of phrase? Fresh icing, even on a stale cake, rewards readers.

John McPhee again, making a point about World War II spurring innovation: "The Second World War was a technological piñata."[28]

Journalist Sheri Fink about hurricanes: "For certain New Orleanians, Memorial Medical Center was the place you went to ride out each hurricane that the loop current of the Gulf of Mexico launched like a pinball at the city."[29]

Neither of these novelties was necessary. Both of them were rewarding. Fink could have penned, "Hurricane Katrina roared ashore with tremendous force." But she knew the value of surprise. Although she could have settled for informing readers, she coined a novel image to engage them.

Make the familiar fresh. When you say something common, be inventive in how you say it.[30] Give readers that tickle on the far side of their unsuspecting minds.

In his essay "A Hanging," George Orwell made the simple act of walking fresh: "At each step his muscles slid neatly into place, the lock of hair on his scalp danced up and down, his feet printed themselves on the wet gravel."

Essayist Christopher Hitchens did the same in describing cancer: "The whole cave of my chest and thorax seemed to have been hollowed out and then refilled with slow-drying cement."[31]

As a warning, you can't make the familiar fresh with common idioms. Say you're tempted to write, "Congress is grasping at straws in the crisis." We know from Rutvik Desai and colleagues that this doesn't get mental traction. The Desai team asked people to read that sentence (among others). They wanted to see how much a verb ("grasp") embedded in a familiar idiom excites motor neurons. Does it spur simulation? Do the circuits for hand motion fire?

The answer was . . . hardly at all. The cliché-like idiom made readers' processing eyes glaze over. Desai and his team's research even suggests you're better off writing with naked verbs than those clothed in cliché. They showed that using "to grasp" in a literal sentence—"The instructor is grasping the steering wheel"—excites more simulation in motor-circuit neurons than "grasp" in the idiom.[32] "Clichés," as a friend of mine says, "are metaphors with rigor mortis."[33] If you want to break open a piñata of new meaning, give readers a tool they don't expect to work with.

Kindle new reactions. By combining words in unorthodox ways, you release new energy by violating the prediction machine. Unexpected combinations—they are a simple tactic to surprise.

Say you're making the case that historians too easily ignore the history of failures. You could say, as Carl Zimmer did, "It's easier . . . to ignore . . . *the fame that curdled.*"[34]

Or say you're profiling a company's working conditions. You could write, "The boss is charismatic but makes you feel subservient." Or as James Baldwin wrote, his father had ". . . *a crushing charm.*"[35]

Or say you're in healthcare and you start, "There's nothing more pivotal to healthy living than a healthy heart." You could instead write, as did Colin and Thomas Campbell, "The heart is the centerpiece of life and, more often than not in America, the centerpiece of death."[36]

The union of unlike elements, or even the uncommon juxtaposition of ordinary ones, brings energy out of each of them. You don't need a big vocabulary. Notice how common words—glittering and misery, fame and curdling, crushing and charm—couple into new, rewarding wholes.

Upend the ordinary. Turn the customary into the creative. For example, can you take a tired expression—"the chickens came home to roost"—and reconfigure it to serve another point, "The chickens roosted to come home"?

Say you simply want to distinguish your message from others. Here's Suzanne Simard in her book *Finding the Mother Tree*: "After a lifetime as a forest detective, my perception of the woods has been turned upside down. . . . This is not a book about how we can save the trees. This is a book about how the trees might save us."[37]

Or say you want to cite your compulsion to solve a vexing question. You could say, "The job consumed me with curiosity." Or, as Jon Franklin, a Pulitzer winner, said, "I itched to know, the way you do when you find yourself in possession of an answer but you don't know what the question was."[38]

Or take issue with conventional wisdom—say, Vince Lombardi's epigram, "Quitters never win and winners never quit." If you're like Seth Godin, a pro in the business press, you play the contrarian: "Bad advice. Winners quit all the time. *They just quit the right stuff at the right time.*"[39]

We learn as kids to delight in such twists. Here's one more, Dorothy in *The Wonderful Wizard of Oz*: "I think you are wrong to want a heart. It makes most people unhappy. If you only knew it, you are in luck not to have a heart."[40]

By upending the ordinary, you have readers' brains going right as you spin left. With that reverse pirouette, as in L. Frank Baum's advice for the Tinman (in the mouth of Dorothy), you engage, maybe even for generations.

Throw a final punch. There's no surprise quite like one held to the end. Do you usually settle for exiting in slippers? Or do you try to depart in ruby shoes? The power position is the parting word, phrase, sentence, or paragraph. To reward and engage, click your heels unexpectedly before you clack that period.[41]

Say you're a scientist, and you're writing about black holes. Here's Chris Impey at the University of Arizona as he ends a paragraph: "Black holes are tombs of matter; nothing can escape them, not even light. . . . As the poet Dante described the words over the gates of hell in his poem 'The Divine Comedy': Abandon hope, all ye who enter here."[42]

You can take inspiration from one of the great pros of all time, Victor Hugo: "I met in the street a very poor young man who was in love. His hat was old, his coat worn, his cloak was out at the elbows, the water passed through his shoes—and the stars through his soul."[43]

You can also simply structure a sentence to save the punch for the last words. William Jacob Holland, in *The Moth Book*, a guide to North American moths: "When the moon shall have faded out from the sky, and the sun shall shine at noonday a dull cherry red, and the seas shall be frozen over, and the icecap shall have crept downward to the equator from either pole . . . when all the cities shall have long been dead and crumbled into dust, and all life shall be on the last verge of extinction on this globe; then, on a bit of lichen, growing on the bald rocks beside the eternal snows of Panama, shall be seated a tiny insect, preening its antennae in the glow of the worn-out sun, the sole survivor of animal life on this our earth—a melancholy bug."[44]

A rule to end this chapter by: If the first sentence that comes to mind won't surprise readers, think up another one. People are wired to hunger for and devour surprise. They yearn to feel the click of the unexpected. As they say in New York publishing, the first thing editors want is novelty. No surprise, no click, no readers.

CHAPTER 4

KEEP IT STIRRING

For the Love of Readers: Have Feeling

Funny thing about words tinged with emotion: People initiate the processing of them faster than neutral words. At least a few percent faster.[1] Or more.[2] Even if the word is abstract. Not only do readers read faster when you use a word that denotes an emotion—"terror," "awe." They read faster for words just colored with emotion—"debt," "marriage."

Sounds incredible, doesn't it? This is because charged words spark processing of the fear or anger or happiness they contain right along with—and often before—people have the chance to process the remainder of the words' meaning. If you write "fire!" your readers react to the emotional content in 200 milliseconds or less. That compares to 400 milliseconds for them to fully access the word's meaning.[3]

"We are not yet aware of the meaning," says Francesca Citron, a psycholinguist and cognitive neuroscientist at Lancaster University in the United Kingdom, "yet already we have a preferential response to emotional-content words, because these words, even though they are symbols, don't demand our full access to the meaning to react to them."[4]

That's how we're wired, thanks to the edge our ancient ancestors needed in acting faster than, in a sense, they could think. The emotional content took priority over the logical content. And that points to the fourth secret to winning over your readers: Compose to take advantage of the logical *and* emotional content of your material.

You might protest: In my writing, I deliver my message from the high ground of the intellect! But scientists say otherwise. You're hardwired by evolution to respond to every hint of emotion. Moreover, you respond to each emotion with a preprogrammed impulse.[5] You can't stop the reflex. You heed the feelings before the facts.

Of course, the emotional and intellectual parts ultimately play together. They work as partners to influence what readers understand. They are like the score of a movie and the script. Acting together, they cue action in different parts of the brain, spike desire, and hold out the promise of pleasure.

Why do authors W. Chan Kim and Renée Mauborgne start their book on business strategy, *Blue Ocean Strategy*, with the line, "A onetime accordion player, stilt walker, and fire eater, Guy Laliberté is now CEO of Cirque du Soleil ..."?[6]

Because in part (whether they knew it or not), by introducing a person and linking him to accordions, stilts, and fire eaters, they surfaced content with emotion. Awe, humor, joy, fear—each emotional allusion sets off neuronal firing. And that firing—from the get-go—spurs off-the-shelf inclinations that influence what readers comprehend.

Which makes sense if you think about it. Tens of thousands of years ago, snap decisions gave humans those extra split seconds on which their survival depended. *Avalanche!* No waiting to process the ins and outs of that word! We're wired to let emotion give us a jump on slower, "full" comprehension that would leave us for dead (or hungry or thirsty or friendless).

EMOTION IN CHARGE

You may never have thought of the impact of language this way. But the electricity of emotion energizes most words' meaning. Only when readers mentally combine the emotional connotation and the informational content do they comprehend the words fully. The effect of the combination governs how readers feel and influences how much you engage and persuade them.

Or to state the inverse: Communicating without emotion stunts your ability to transform your writing to better connect with readers. No emotion on your part, no full comprehension on theirs. Facts and feelings are incomplete without their marriage. They resonate as one.

Research by Citron at Lancaster University confirms this. "When you read language with emotion, you are more likely to pay attention, keep reading, keep focused, keep processing for a prolonged period of time, because the text grabs your attention," she says. "Emotion helps to engage you, and you are less likely to get bored and stop reading."

Professional writers know this from experience. Take a passage from Carlos Eire, writing with words full of emotion about his childhood in Cuba: "On hot tropical nights . . . there were too many parties to count. Rum, limes, beer, loud music that unmasked veiled mysteries, and far too many cigarettes. Shouting, sweating, dancing, whispering, and far too many hands, hips, and lips on forbidden places. And prayers, too. Always."[7]

Rum, cigarettes, whispering, hips, forbidden. You probably don't get such racy material to work with, but Eire's example helps you see—feel—how emotion-laden words hold on to your mind. The words do so in this case not just because they are specific—which of course drives a flurry of simulation.[8] Their emotional content combines with their literal definition to trigger a sort of spontaneous combustion of meaning. And it's the heat of that combustion that wins over readers.

The specific emotion you experience comes, of course, from the context in which you learned the words. The word "limes," for example, might convey to you a feeling of comfort from, say, memories of picking them with your big brother. Or it might reprise a feeling of love from having watched your mother slice them for drinks. Or it might evoke a feeling of disgust from recalling the time you bit into one and spit out the bitter citrus.

Most words come to you with a common history, however, one you share with other people. In an experiment with 175 ordinary words, for example, researchers tracked common emotional associations. Not surprisingly, the top words readers linked to joy were "sun," "sea," and "summer." The top-rated ones for anger: "traffic jam," "arrogance," and "greed."[9] This emotional charge is what you want to be aware of—and take advantage of.

How does the emotion in language affect the brain itself? The emotional content, to simplify a bit, gets processed initially in the brain's amygdala. Within 100 milliseconds or so of reading or hearing stirring words, the amygdala sends

signals across other parts of your brain and from your brain
through your body. You then feel the emergence of a bodily
sensation—the heat in your chest, the tension in your neck . . .
or chills from joy. The physiological reaction marks the point,
in scientific terms, when an emotion in the mind becomes a
conscious feeling.

The specific conscious feeling varies depending on the
commands from the brain: Secrete stress hormones into the
blood. Contract the muscles. Accelerate breathing. Speed
the heart rate. Deploy the goose bumps. That's when the
reward circuit, detecting a reaction in the body, makes judgments: Is this good or bad? Pleasant or unpleasant? Is this
stimulus something I should pursue? Avoid?[10]

Emotions thereby step up the urgency and potency of
language processing.[11] Readers may not even sense the neural impact early on. A team at Carnegie Mellon University,
however, showed that each emotion, from disgust to lust to
happiness, produces a unique neural signature.[12] This is what's
key: The related bodily sensations, not just the neural firing in
the brain, contribute to readers' language processing—even if
this is sometimes initially subconscious.

KNOW IT OR NOT

So when you mess with words weighted with emotion, you
mess with people's minds *and* bodies. To get a sense for how
interrelated emotion and language are, consider research by
Arash Aryani and colleagues at Freie Universität Berlin. They
had people read both real and fake emotionally laden words
and then score them as either positive or negative. They made

sure the fake ones, called pseudowords, *sounded* real owing to sounds similar to real words. But the fakers, from a language point of view, were meaningless.

What Aryani and his colleagues found was that words with short vowels (akin to barks) scored as more arousing, "arousal" being a neuroscientist's measure of emotional intensity. So did words with "voiceless stops" (*t* or *k*)—which of course includes words not spoken in pleasant company. And so did words with hissing sounds, "produced by a high-velocity jet of air against the teeth." They found that it didn't matter if the words were real or fake; the barks, stops, and hisses scored high on unpleasantness.

So we can guess that even before we as humans communicated with words, we made meaning with our voices. Grunts and gasps naturally would have predated language. Our brains, as a result, give emotional weighting, often just from the sound of words, first hearing and then processing the literal connotation. Aryani and his team made their point with the title of their article: "Why 'Piss' Is Ruder Than 'Pee'?"[13]

One question for writers is this: How much priority does the brain give to emotional words? Does it matter so much that I should worry about it? The answer is yes, and the explanation comes from a classic experiment: Ordinarily, if you listen to someone read a list of words, you need a moment to orient your attention to each one. You invariably miss a few because of what scientists dub the "attentional blink." That's when you hit an attentional limit. You can digest only so much so fast.

But there's an exception to the blink: When the word is emotionally significant. You then *do not* experience the blink.

You *do* notice the word.[14] It doesn't matter if the emotion is positive or negative. So strong is the neural power of emotion that it's hard to ignore it. Emotion grabs you by the collar.

The research on the attentional blink instantly raises another question. If emotional words have the advantage of getting preemptive notice, positive or negative, do they also have the advantage of prompting reward, positive or negative? Separate research gives us an affirmative answer, which might at first seem counterintuitive.

But how could that be? Why would your reward circuit trigger desire and even hold out the promise of pleasure for, say, words that express anger or disgust? The suggestion by scientists is that this again comes from an evolutionary advantage. When our ancestors heeded bad things, however disagreeable, they reaped just as big a payoff in their ability to survive and thrive as for good things.

To reveal the effect, Rajendra Badgaiyan at State University of New York at Buffalo scanned people's brains as they read negative words, like "fire" and "blood," as well as neutral ones, "park" and "pencil." Comparing the two, he could see that, with negative emotional words, dopamine moved from the amygdala to other parts of the reward circuit. The dopamine didn't flow along the same pathway as for pleasant words, which reveals the complexity of the reward circuit's microwiring. But the motivating effect of the signal was just the same.[15]

Vincent Costa and others at the University of Florida investigated people's reaction to texts instead of just words. They asked 29 students to silently read 42 different 12-second narratives, some pleasant, some unpleasant. After each one, they asked the students to keep imagining the scene while an fMRI scanned their brains. Here's an example of a pleasant story: "It's the last few minutes of the big game and it's close. The crowd explodes in a deafening roar. You jump up, cheering. Your team has come from behind to win."

Here's an unpleasant one: "A night landing in high winds: Your hands clutch the seat-arms in the swaying plane. Stomach queasy. The engine coughs; stops; restarts with a strange whine."

Costa's team, like Badgaiyan, found that neurotransmitters traveled two different pathways, but both drove the reward circuit.[16] That raises the question for writers: Just how unpleasant can your words get before you turn off people's reward circuit? When does negative emotion snuff out the circuit's motivating effect? Where do you draw the line if you need to use negative emotion to engage people? Will an emotional gut punch turn readers off?

Suzanne Oosterwijk and others at the University of Amsterdam wondered about the same questions. So they asked people to read descriptions of pleasant pictures—"Children throw flower petals at a wedding"—and then click "yes" or "no" if they wanted to see the pictures. They also asked them to read unpleasant descriptions—"A soldier kicks a civilian in the head"—and click to see the pictures as well.

They theorized that people would interpret negative descriptions as a cue to more "novel, rare, deviant, uncertain, challenging, or complex" information. The higher learning value of that information, they theorized, would prompt people to hit the "yes" button. At this point, at the time of button press, it wouldn't matter if they later liked the images or not and experienced pleasure—that was another question.

True to their theory, they found that people not only chose to see 81 percent of the negative images (versus 95 percent of the positive ones). They also found, in scans, that people experienced a neural pattern for the negative cues that was roughly the same as for the positive ones. Moreover, the negative cues (stories) fired reward regions more strongly than the positive ones.[17] So the reward circuit, apparently with little hesitation, sensed a learning opportunity and thus kept up its motivating power.

Which doesn't mean that scientists have found that gory stuff trumps nice stuff. The cues just made people *want* to see the pictures. It spiked desire. That delivered some pleasure at the incentive phase—regardless of whether people got turned off later—when they saw the picture. The results highlight just how much the motivating phases of the reward circuit—wanting, liking, and learning—separately contribute to reward-driven behavior. The first does not necessarily lead to the second or third.[18] They can each have their own impact.

So, as a writer, you don't have to shun horrid material. It rewards people—at least as far as spiking desire. When you flesh out the writing, though, you need to draw the line on what's appropriate. What kinds of emotional material are sensible versus senseless, needed versus needless, engaging versus repellent? You may find that the reward of negative emotion, however motivating, comes from the buildup and not from the delivery.

MIND TO BODY AND BACK

The power of emotion in words comes, of course, from both simulation in the mind and simulation in the body. To get an idea of how far the effect extends, Edita Fino and colleagues at the University of Bologna asked people to read simple statements with verbs with positive emotions—"Mario smiles" and "Mario enjoys." They meanwhile measured the microvoltage change in the principal cheek muscle for smiling (the "zygomaticus major").

They wondered: How much will action verbs (e.g., "smile") and "state" verbs (e.g., "enjoy") differ in triggering muscle action? Though people reading were unaware of it, both verbs activated their smile muscles (in this case, more so for the state verbs after 300 milliseconds and the action verbs after a second or so). When people were asked to read negative statements—"Mario scowls" and "Mario gets angry"—people engaged the frown muscles between the eyes (the "corrugator supercilia").

The scientists made two points, which reinforce what we've learned up to this point. The first was that the microvoltage pop they recorded reflected, initially, a response by facial neurons in the brain and, almost in parallel, a muscular simulation in the face. The second is that the muscle action, coming so fast, helped people grasp the meaning. Comprehension wasn't all in the head. It was boosted by signals buzzing back from the body.[19]

Alessandra Vergallito at the University of Milano-Bicocca and others ran a similar experiment that then went further. They tracked facial muscles as people listened to random emotion-laden words—"bankrupt," "suffocate," "relaxed," "passion," "pizza," "home," "victory." They then measured heart rate and tracked action in the upper lip-raising muscle ("levator labii"). That muscle is linked to sadness, disgust, and fear.

They found people's heart rates rose a beat or two per minute for the positive words. What's more, not only voluntary muscles were getting into the word-processing game. The involuntary ones were, too—and this for words that were both concrete ("pizza") and abstract ("passion").[20]

Another question was raised by this research: *Must* people use their muscles to comprehend? What would happen if our muscles were unable to participate? Would it matter? A team led by David Havas at the University of Wisconsin, Madison, devised an experiment to come up with an answer. They alternately enhanced or hindered readers' muscle actions to see what happened to the speed of comprehension.

To control facial muscles, they used a simple trick. They asked people to hold a pen in their teeth. In clenching a pen, people's cheek muscles (the zygomaticus) get forced into a smile. They asked people at other times to hold the pen in their lips. In pursing the pen, people's brow muscles (corrugators) get forced into a frown or pout. The pen trick assured that the team alternately induced either a happy or irritating facial-muscle posture.

People then read 48 pleasant and 48 unpleasant sentences. For example, "You and your lover embrace after a long separation." Or, "The police car rapidly pulls up behind you, siren blaring." It turned out that people read the pleasant sentences 54 milliseconds faster with pens in their teeth (smiling) than with pens in their lips (frowning). They read the unpleasant sentences 36 milliseconds slower. The reverse setup yielded the reverse results.[21]

The suggestion from this correlation is remarkable: If you can't get your facial muscles to help, you process emotion-laden sentences slower. Havas then did himself one better. He wondered: Do the muscles *cause* better comprehension? With another team, he partnered with plastic surgeons to recruit 41 women signed up to have Botox treatments to clear up their frowns. The patients were in a special position to help with Havas's question. That's because botulinum toxin-A paralyzes the frown muscles. The treatment, in other words, provided a convenient juncture to deactivate the women's mind-body action during comprehension.

The women were offered $50 discounts if they chose to join the new study. Before and after their Botox injection, they read 60 sad, angry, and happy sentences. Havas and his team theorized, as you can guess, that if their facial muscles did help with understanding emotion-laden sentences, the Botoxed women would take slightly longer to understand the sad and angry ones. You can see where this is going.

Imagine for a moment reading the same sentences as the women. An angry one: "Reeling from the fight with that stubborn bigot, you slam the car door." A sad one: "You hold back your tears as you enter the funeral home." A happy one: "Finally, you reach the summit of the tall mountain." What was the difference when the Botoxed women were reading? It took 200 milliseconds longer for them to understand sad and angry sentences.

Paralyzing the frown muscle did indeed *cause* slower comprehension.[22] This research, along with other experiments that confirm causation,[23] again supports the notion that you can use emotion to put muscle in your prose. In that you normally feel the same emotion composing a sentence as a reader does reading it, the feeling you get in your muscles or gut while coming up with a word is likely the same one readers will get. You can use your personal emotional barometer to guide you when writing.

Now if you're writing a persuasive argument, you'll probably want to know the answer to another question: Does priming people with emotional words affect their judgment? That is, does it affect not just comprehension, but decision-making? Francesco Foroni and Gün Semin of VU University Amsterdam and the University of Utrecht tackled that question. They primed people with emotional words—"grin," "cry," "irritating"—to see how that influenced their opinions of cartoons.

The emotional words flashed for 30 milliseconds on a screen, a subliminal prime, too brief to see consciously. Afterward, people judged cartoons on a nine-point scale—not at all funny, extremely so, something in between. The result was that people who saw positive verbs (e.g., "laugh," "grin") rated the cartoons as much funnier than people who saw negative ones (e.g., "cry," "squeal"). This confirmed emotional priming distorts people's judgment. And if you're one of those people, you have no idea the prime swayed your decision.[24]

You can get the idea that practicing the keep-it-stirring strategy is akin to practicing reader manipulation. That's of course a fair conclusion. You can see the potential for abuse. (Politicians do it all the time.) On the other hand, you can also see the potential for more fully rewarding readers with important information. People understand you better when you leaven plain language with an emotion, which can further—and not distort—meaning.

FORCE OF NATURE

Writing with emotion has many practical benefits. Along with processing emotional words faster than other words, people also process them more accurately.[25] They remember them better, as well, because facts and feeling get encoded together.

In a simple experiment to see how much emotion affects memory, Jeanette Altarriba and Lisa Bauer at the State University of New York at Albany and Syracuse University asked people to listen to lists of 20 words each, one list abstract, one concrete, and one with emotion. Afterward, people wrote down as many words as they could recall. On average, after sessions with each list, people could recall about six abstract words, eight concrete ones, and nine with emotion. Emotion, in other words, trumps concreteness as a memory aide. "Thrilled" and "anxious," as part of a list, are more memorable than words like "airplane" and "scissors."[26]

This seems at odds with the research on the concreteness effect from chapter 2. And it's puzzling at first. But researchers say that emotional words bring up more images from memories linked to them (slicing limes). That makes them easier to simulate and, as a hidden benefit, to remember.

Emotion also has the advantage of keeping people reading. Once again, Jonah Berger and colleagues highlighted how big an advantage. They studied 827,000 online reading sessions by readers of 39,000 news articles. Articles came from nine online publishers, among them CNBC, ESPN, *The Wall Street Journal,* and Gizmodo. By crunching data with natural language processing, they wanted to see what kind of text in each paragraph kept people reading to the next paragraph.

They found that emotional text ranked high. Positive emotions in one paragraph boosted the probability of people reading further by 3.9 percent. Negative emotions did the same, anger lifting the probability by 3.5 percent and anxiety 4.9 percent. The sole exception to the emotion-boosting effect was sadness, which cut further reading by 6.8 percent.[27]

Ahmed Al-Rawi at Concordia University found similar results. He tracked the "most retweeted" 200 stories in four top newspapers. More than half of stories (58 percent) retweeted have positive emotions and less than half negative (42 percent). The most common positive emotion? Awe (58 percent of stories). The most common negative ones? Anger (29 percent) and anxiety (14 percent).[28] That positive news stories so often go viral contrasts with popular thinking that the news media win over readers only with negative news.

We can guess that the exercise in which researchers changed the names of menu items at the University of Illinois faculty cafeteria (see the beginning of chapter 2) demonstrates more than the power of specifics. It also shows how much emotion-laden language changes people's decisions. Brian Wansink and others inferred that they could trigger emotional memories of family, tradition, and country by, for instance, changing "Zucchini Cookies" into "Grandma's Zucchini Cookies." They speculated that the emotional tie partly explained the 27 percent jump in sales of such relabeled food.[29]

Even what seems like a trivial emotional trigger can affect reader response. David Havas (again) and Christopher Chapp took a unique approach to look into the subtleties. They compared verb tenses used in 148 stump speeches from the 2012 presidential campaign with 48 State of the Union speeches from earlier presidents. The State of the Union texts ranged from Lyndon Johnson's speech in 1965 to Barack Obama's in 2013.

The subtle difference they measured: how often the presidents used the past perfect versus the past imperfect. They theorized that people would comprehend the past perfect as referring to a completed act—been-there-done-that history. By contrast, the past imperfect would be understood to refer to an incomplete act—one that's ongoing—been-there-and-still-doing-that history.

Here's an example of the past perfect: "Families struggled to make the mortgage." You can hear how the action, an emotional one, is finished. And the past imperfect: "Families were struggling to make the mortgage." You can see how the action, though pictured as happening in the past, is still ongoing. Havas and Chapp theorized that the past imperfect would coax readers into more simulation and thus intensify the emotional impact.

Readers confirmed that the scientists were probably right. Readers of passages from stump speeches rated the past imperfect ones as more emotionally intense. These people, who had no idea why they were being asked, cited feelings with the past imperfect ranging from "afraid" and "angry" to "excited" and "happy." *The verb tense alone* made that difference.

The presidents and their speechwriters apparently understood intuitively that they'd work up their audience more surely by taking advantage of the emotion implicit in the imperfect: The stump speeches used more than four times as many (adjusted for length) imperfect conjugations as in the state of the union speeches. The past imperfect was working like a subliminal prime, helping audiences feel engaged and politicians get elected (if not liked afterward).[30]

EMOTIONAL ADVICE

The research makes it more than clear: Emotions of even the most subtle kind reel in your audience. Bare-bones logic, although powerful, does not win as surely without a warm body of feeling to go with it. As Nobelist Daniel Kahneman said after decades of investigating the rational and irrational sides of human thinking, "The emotional tail wags the rational dog."[31]

So if you're a writer, what is the right balance of emotions? One theory, dating to Aristotle, argues that people most like to feel the "right" ones.[32] And what does *that* mean? It means you have to judge from experience, not from any rules I can give you, on how to align the emotional tail and dog. Science can help you see the implication of your words, but it can't prescribe them.

For writers trained to stress logic above all—engineers, lawyers, scientists, policy wonks—the question is probably not so much how to shoehorn emotion into your writing. It is breaking the habit of freezing it out. If you exile emotion, you probably risk writing tedious prose that even your friends and colleagues may find foreign.

The trick is calibrating your presentation of fact and feeling so they resonate as a bona fide whole with your audience. A bit of energy for what you're saying, if just palpable enthusiasm, helps readers grasp your meaning. You then give readers the feeling—your feeling—that the hard edge of logic and soft touch of emotion are "just right." Here are four tactics to help you meet that challenge:

Have attitude. Convey conviction. If you work on a piece of writing you care about, you should be able to show it. Get readers to feel what you feel.

After taking potshots at Charles Darwin in the first chapter, I come back to him to show how he ended *On the Origin of Species*: "And as natural selection works solely by and for the good of each being. . . . Thus, from the war of nature, from famine and death, the most exalted object which we are capable of conceiving, namely, the production of the higher animals, directly follows. There is grandeur in this view of life . . . from so simple a beginning endless forms most beautiful and most wonderful have been, and are being evolved."[33]

Okay, the text is dated. But you can see how even Darwin, with zeal for his theory, uses loaded words ("famine," "grandeur") and projected awe. He arguably weighted his words with the "right" emotion to move you at the magnificence of his discovery. His facts informed feeling and feelings informed facts. To develop the attitude that will work for you, ask: What feeling did I have when committing to this writing project in the first place?

As Henry David Thoreau said, "Write while the heat is in you. The writer who postpones the recording of his thoughts uses an iron which has cooled to burn a hole with. He cannot inflame the minds of his audience."[34]

Physician Atul Gawande summoned the right attitude when he wrote *Being Mortal,* his book about gaps in healthcare for the elderly. He could have written without heat: "Long-term care facilities for the elderly are not up to the task for the future. . . ." But he wrote: "You'd think people would have rebelled. You'd think we would have burned the nursing homes to the ground. We haven't, though, because we find it hard to believe that anything better is possible. . . ."[35]

You don't have to whip people up. But you can choose words so that the script and score resonate to boost the reader's comprehension. And while you're at it, err on the side of finishing on an up beat. We know from experimental data that sentences with positive emotions are processed faster.[36] At the close, rise above the negative. Exit with the grandeur of Darwin.

Frame feeling. Choose words and phrases that frame your feeling to guide readers in interpreting your message. Your emotional frame, as much as your logical one, dictates your meaning.

Consider how a diverse, Texas-based conglomerate described itself in a 2016 shareholder letter: "Think of Biglari Holdings as a museum of businesses. Our preference is to collect masterpieces."[37] Chairman of the Board Sardar Biglari linked business to awe-inspiring institutions full of treasures. That frame guided investors in interpreting his company's progress.

A caution: Frames easily manipulate readers wrongfully. You can use them to lead as well as mislead readers. Psychologist Amos Tversky, Kahneman's longtime colleague, showed in a classic experiment at Harvard Medical School that just swapping frames—without changing the facts—can even *reverse* meaning.

Tversky gave physicians statistics on five-year outcomes for lung-cancer treatments. Some patients had received surgery, some radiation. Half the doctors got data on what Tversky labeled as "survival" rates for surgery—"The one-month survival rate is 90%." The other half got "mortality" rates for surgery—"There is a 10% mortality in the first month." Opposite frames, same data.

He then asked doctors: Which treatment would you prefer for patients? Eighty-four percent of the doctors favored surgery to radiation when they got survival rates. Fifty percent favored radiation when the outcomes were expressed as mortality rates.[38] To the chagrin of most champions of facts and data: Even the most analytic of professionals follow the emotional frame when making life-or-death decisions.

David Hauser and Megan Fleming at Queen's University in Toronto asked people to evaluate the impact of hurricanes. They framed the severity of the storms for different readers with either literal words or "antagonist" figurative language. An excerpt of their text: "Nags Head [North Carolina] will soon feel Hurricane Lee's arrival [or alternately] fury." "When hurricanes are framed as antagonists," write the authors, "people forecast more lives lost, more homes destroyed, more days without power, and a more severe storm." The people also said they would be more likely to evacuate.[39]

"Survival" versus "mortality," "arrival" versus "fury," "businesses" versus "masterpieces"—scientists confirm that the
emotional frame molds meaning in readers' minds. The next
time you email people to schedule a meeting for, say, a de-
briefing on a project screwup, what will you call it? A post-
mortem? An investigation of accountability? A root-cause
analysis? A celebration of learning?

Move with metaphor. Why use a metaphor if a literal
expression says the same thing? Because metaphors convey
feeling (not to mention surprise, simulation, and more).[40]

Say you're giving advice to another person on how to do
a job performance review. You could say, "Praise the person
first to soften the impact of finding fault." Or you could, as
did Dale Carnegie in *How to Win Friends and Influence People,*
"Beginning with praise is like the dentist who begins his
work with Novocain. The patient still gets a drilling, but . . ."[41]

Or say you're Steve Calandrillo, a University of Washington
law professor, writing an essay on the benefits of staying on
daylight savings time year-round. You could write, "Crime
increases after darkness." Calandrillo wrote, "Darkness is . . . a
friend of crime."[42]

Or say you're writing an op-ed. You could start: "One failing of our justice system is that it often works to jail minor of-
fenders and let the worst criminals go free." That's a perfectly
fine sentence. But consider this classic line from Jonathan
Swift: "Laws are like cobwebs, which may catch small flies,
but let wasps and hornets break through."[43]

Metaphor and figurative language—novocaine, darkness,
hornets—stir readers at the gut level because they invariably come with tails of emotion. The words, the images, the

context, the sensations evoked—their feeling wags the logic one way or another to help people get your point fully.

That certainly explains why you see so many metaphors in political speech. A team led by Vinodkumar Prabhakaran at Google Research showed how popular figurative flourishes are. They used natural language processing to analyze 85,000 Facebook posts by 412 politicians in 2017. The metaphor-rich posts—often using the simplest turns of phrase, namely "jumpstart the economy" as opposed to "improve the economy"—sparked more "participation," "acceptance," and "propagation."[44] In other words, they engaged.

Move with people. There's no easier way to evoke emotion among readers than to put people in your prose. That allows you to present winners, losers, instigators, irritants, entertainers, gadflies, popularizers, and more. The people and their situation act as emotional triggers.

Why did Simon Sinek start *Leaders Eat Last* with, "A thick layer of clouds blocked out any light. There were no stars and there was no moon. Just black. The team slowly made its way through the valley . . ."?[45]

And why did Siddhartha Mukherjee start *The Emperor of All Maladies: A Biography of Cancer* with: "On the morning of May 19, 2004, Carla Reed, a 30-year-old kindergarten teacher from Ipswich, Massachusetts, a mother of three young children, woke up in bed with a headache. 'Not just any headache,' she would recall later, 'but a sort of numbness in my head . . .'"?[46]

And why did Andrea Rock open her book on dreaming, *The Mind at Night*, with: "By the time Eugene Aserinsky found himself in a dungeon-like lab room . . . wiring his eight-year-old son, Armond, with electrodes to record his eye movements and brain waves as he slept, he was desperate. The experiment he was embarking upon absolutely had to work so that he could finally earn his degree and get a job"?[47]

Because with those openings, they could engage you by amplifying emotions in people who must obviously be having them. Even if you make up characters, you can highlight their pleasures and plights. An emotionally lifeless topic, like a new technology, once brought to life by someone struck by fortune or misfortune, arouses readers.

Many writers worry as Mark Twain did: "We all do no end of feeling, and we mistake it for thinking."[48] Twain was right. You can write too much from the gut and too little from the brain. That's not something you want to be known for if you seek to break out with influence in any profession. You lose if you're seen as being wagged by an emotional tail.

But if you're intellectually driven, the risk of shortchanging readers in comprehending you fully without wagging any tail at all is greater. Seeking the "right" combination of "hot" language (with emotion) and "cold" (logic) promises to reward readers as you would yourself. Your readers don't want to get an emotional drilling. But neither do they want to lose feeling under the influence of novocaine.

CHAPTER 5

KEEP IT SEDUCTIVE

For the Love of Readers: Arouse Anticipation

Remember as a child how you would get so excited about the smallest things? Enough to bounce on your toes over the prospects of, say, the Tooth Fairy? That sure was pleasant, wasn't it? Fact is, for most us, it still is. We may no longer bounce on our toes, of course.

The fifth secret to winning over readers is to reward them with the pleasure of anticipation. Get them to stick with you by signaling that you'll soon give them something good—maybe great—to induce at least a little of that old toe-bouncing feeling.

Professional writers use this tactic all the time. Wallace Stegner, in his chronicle of John Wesley Powell's 1870 boat trip through the Grand Canyon, wrote that the Powell brothers "represented military discipline and the officer class, and . . . the men who were to accompany them represented frontier independence and a violent distaste for discipline of any kind."[1]

A distaste for discipline of any kind. You can't help but want to learn more. What does the future hold for the Powells—a war-psychotic ex-captain and a one-armed ex-major of artillery—in managing this independent crew on a section of the Colorado River? How will their relationship play out with free-minded frontiersmen and trappers?

You can see how evolution would have wired your brain to enjoy anticipating the answer. You are then motivated to keep reading, and not just by the prospect of consuming the outcome. You're motivated to stick around for the pleasure of the period beforehand. Looking forward to the reward, you stand by faithfully until that act of consumption.

As we now know from scientific experiments, that initial waiting period *increases* your total pleasure. Yes, that's correct. And it doesn't matter what the stimulus is. Even before you read what happened on the Colorado River—or even before you buy that donut at the coffee shop—your reward circuit motivates you by ginning up desire and imparting pleasure.

This is counterintuitive. The acts of consuming *and* contemplating consumption have payoffs? Yes, it's true. You savor in advance—almost foolishly—the desire and pleasure of hoping for . . . well, for more savoring later. Which explains why studies show that people routinely report just as much happiness in the period looking forward to a vacation as they do after they get back.[2] The glow of going away starts *before* you leave home.

For writers, the point is that readers sensing a shred of beneficial information coming down the line experience desire and even pleasure before they get it. So much so, according to studies, that even the promise of information with no value at

all engages the reward circuit. Anticipation for any information, in other words, is its own reward.[3]

CURIOUS AROUSAL

You may think winning over readers by keeping it seductive is fine for writers like Stegner. A tale about explorers
and outlaws—that's an easy sell. But what about dry subjects,
subjects in law or business or medicine? Research shows that
the same principle applies. You don't even need to feature
interesting people to make it work. You can still get readers'
look-ahead juices flowing.

As an example, here's Marco Magnani, an economist, writing about the "dismal science": "One rarely goes to a museum
to find a model of how to stimulate local economic development. That's particularly true in Florence, Italy, where you
instead go to see treasures by Botticelli, da Vinci, Raphael,
Caravaggio, and Titian. But Florence has a noted exception if
you're an economist: the Palazzo Strozzi . . . [and how it uses]
art to stimulate economic development."[4]

Magnani, an academic, plays to your toe-bouncing impulses just like author Stegner. He makes you wonder: What
are the good things in store to learn about in the Palazzo? So
strong is the impulse to pursue the answer that it can get the
better of you not just when you know you'll find the information useful. It can win you over even for information as
useless as trivia.

As an example, take these questions: In what country did
carving jack-o'-lanterns originate? Which rodent doesn't have

a tail? What year was Lady Gaga born? What was the first toy advertised on television?

Are you anticipating the answers? If you're like most people, you're hungry to gobble them up, piddling though their value may be. Your reward circuit is driving that hunger. You may even feel the pleasant heat of anticipatory desire. That desire in part reflects the evolutionary drive wired into your brain to continuously update your grasp of reality, or as scientists say, your neural models of the outside world.

Another name for this impulse is curiosity. Curiosity about the big and essential questions in life. Or the silly and shallow. You had that curiosity drilled into the function of your brain over millennia. You may thus even get more reward from seeking information—the anticipation—than from the delivery.[5] Scientists call this form of reward "anticipatory utility."[6]

Never mind that many things we want to consume lack an ounce of nutrition—trivia answers like Ireland, guinea pigs, 1986, and Mr. Potato Head. The expected acquisition of promising things seduces us. We are sucked in by that promise in good writing in the same way we are for the expected acquisition of French fries and ice cream. The dopamine in the reward circuit drives us along.

THE THRILL OF WAITING

How do scientists know that mere anticipation turns people on? In a classic experiment in 1987, University of Chicago economist George Loewenstein asked 30 students how much they would pay to immediately consume five different good and bad outcomes. The highlight among the good ones was the chance to obtain a kiss from a movie star of their choice. He also asked how much extra people would pay to wait a bit before consuming each one.[7]

Think about that: How much extra would you pay if, say, you had a guaranteed voucher to get a kiss from your Hollywood heartthrob, but in addition you could exercise the option to put it off? How much more would you pay for waiting a day? Three days? More? How highly would you value the period of delay itself beyond the later action of consuming the kiss?

In line with many studies since, the students consistently said they would pay extra if they could wait a day. They would pay more if they could wait three days. Apparently, the students came up with the answer "by feel," learned from a lifetime of listening to their reward circuits. They knew they would boost their pleasure by opting for a deferral. The frontal part of their brain, the region responsible for valuing payoffs, was telling them they would maximize their *overall* pleasure by waiting.

Remember the last time you decided to save the final piece of cake today so you could eat it tomorrow? That was your reward circuit talking. As Loewenstein points out, people know that the outcome we consume right away may be delightful, but it is fleeting. Our brains then complete a straightforward calculation: We will get more out of this fleeting pleasure by adding the rewards of anticipation to it beforehand. It's elementary math.

Loewenstein's work, however, did show that students hit a limit. After three days, the premium they would pay started falling. They were still urged by their reward circuits to capture the joy of waiting *plus* consumption. They even said they would still pay a little bit more for waiting *an entire year*. But the anticipatory utility fell off over time.

Since Loewenstein's work, some researchers have looked into what happens when they ask people to wait to see pictures merely promised to be appealing.[8] Others have asked people to wait to find out the results of money-winning gambles.[9] Yet others have withheld smiley faces for a period of anticipation after people earned them by correctly identifying images.[10] In all of these cases, the brain components at the heart of the reward circuit lit up before the delivery.

The signature component is a cheese curl–shaped region that arches over the central part of the reward circuit called the caudate nucleus. For simplicity, you can think of the caudate as the anticipation center. When someone withholds payoffs while making promises to deliver them, it's the caudate that guides your response. The caudate in a sense tricks you into playing a game of hard to get. As in other parts of life, getting taken by that game can make your reward circuitry glow.[11]

The sequence of brain activity that creates anticipation stems from your brain working as that prediction engine described in chapter 3. A writing cue drives your desire to know more. That desire impels you to check your memories for what you know from the past. Your past allows you to predict what's ahead. Your predictions prompt you to assess the cues for value. Your assessments allow you to savor the prospect of that value—to savor the period of desire before the payoff.[12]

That further explains why pleasure driven by readers' reward circuitry peaks several seconds *before* peaks in the flow of language. In experiments with poems, people experience emotional highs before the end of emphatic lines and stanzas.

They have learned from experience that poets offer the biggest payoffs at that point, so that's when their anticipation surges. Amazingly, the experiments, led by language researcher Eugen Wassiliwizky and a team from Germany, showed that not just poetry lovers experience this effect. The preemptive spiking of reward is universal, even for readers who have no earlier interest in poetry.[13]

You can see how you could take advantage of this principle even in workaday writing. Say you're writing about town planning. You could start, "The first lesson town planners learn is that they need to upgrade their technology." Or you could start instead: "An unfortunate incident in traffic control holds three lessons for town planners, one about technology, one about politics, and a third about crisis management."

Instead of just stating your message—which is a good thing to start—you amp up the rewards for your readers by outlining but delaying your message. You also amp them up by promising a story about an unfortunate incident. Readers start to enjoy the prospects of payoffs before they get to them. Poetry this is not. But like a poet, you can hold on to readers by signaling the imminent arrival of rich rewards. You can also spur suspense that way, creating a period of "hopeful or anxious anticipation," as scientists say. Or you can spur suspense as you get readers to wonder how you'll update their beliefs about reality.[14]

HOPE REWARDS

You might wonder how scientists separate the rewards of anticipation from the rewards of the delivery of an expected payoff. Investigating that distinction brings us back to trivia. By definition, trivia test the extreme case: How much reward can you stimulate with a promise of information with no "instrumental" value, that is, no usefulness in making anyone's life better? How much anticipatory utility can you manufacture from an initial period of curiosity?

In an early experiment to answer this question, researcher Min Jeong Kang and others asked California Institute of Technology students to read trivia questions like, "What instrument was invented to sound like a human singing?" They then quizzed the students: "How curious are you?" And then, "How confident are you" of knowing the answer? They tracked, in fMRI scans, students' brain activity.

Their data showed that the reward circuit got hooked on anticipating answers with no value at all. The stronger the curiosity, the stronger the effect. Kang's team also tracked readers' pupil dilation. They knew from previous work that the more curiosity elicited in readers, the more their pupils would widen, evidence of arousal in the reward circuit. They found that the widening started five seconds *before* the answer was given. It peaked a second after. The experiment confirmed that curiosity alone—in this case about a violin—spurred the early flow of rewards. It didn't matter that the reward of the answer itself paled in comparison to the period of curiosity.[15]

If you're like me, you find it hard to believe anticipation can make such a difference. To further grasp its power to engage, consider the work of a team led by Johnny King L. Lau at the University of Reading (UK). Lau's team took a different approach to gauge the motivational power of anticipation. They displayed the trivia question, then asked readers how curious they were, and then asked people if they wanted to gamble to find out the answer. The gambling students got to digitally spin the "wheel of fortune." Their willingness to gamble, of course, was a measure of their motivation.

They had to be strongly motivated, too, to spin the wheel. That's because there was a catch. If they won, they would get a sought-after token worth a chance at the end of the experiment to learn the answer. But if they lost, they got the reverse, a token committing them to receiving an electric shock. So, you have to wonder, would these 32 people be motivated to gamble? How motivated would you be, given that researchers had carefully attached menacing electrodes to your body and left them secured spin after spin?

The results gave the answer: Students often took the gamble, even though they also had the choice of avoiding any shocks by not gambling at all. Remarkably, they risked a shock for satisfying their curiosity for useless information. And they did so routinely. Lau's team could meanwhile see the neural firing in people's reward circuits in fMRI scans. If the students decided to spin the wheel, their reward circuits lit up *in advance* of their decision. If they did not, their reward circuits were quiet.

So distinct were the scan results that researchers could *predict* the students' decisions.[16] The anticipation stemming from the mere promise of information drove their decision-making. What does this mean for writing? The stronger the sense of anticipation you build into your writing, the stronger your readers' urge to keep reading. Of course, it also helps if you're writing to a curious audience.

HUMAN HOOKS

You can't assume, however, that even naturally curious readers will brim with curiosity. Research by some scientists shows that you have to trigger it. Readers won't enjoy a period of early rewards if you don't set them up for it. A team led by psychologist Christopher Hsee at the University of Chicago did an experiment to show how this works. They asked groups of people to read a short biography of Albert Einstein. The first group prepared by reading 10 questions about Einstein (e.g., "When was Einstein born?"). The second looked first at 10 pictures of Einstein. The third got to choose which of the first two procedures to follow.

Hsee and his team were explicitly piquing people's curiosity in the first group. The second two groups served for comparison. All the answers to the questions were in the biography. This is what's interesting for writers: When it comes to figuring out which group got the most reward from the biography, the team sampled all the readers' happiness before and after reading. That showed that the first group enjoyed themselves more than the second or third.

What's surprising is that the third group—in spite of having a choice of procedures and the chance to add to their overall pleasure—normally chose to skip the questions. Without the guiding hand of the experimenters, they lost out on receiving rewards from anticipation because they didn't get a setup to pique their curiosity. They unwittingly enjoyed themselves less.[17] The lesson for writers is that you can reward readers with the pleasure of anticipation, but you have to structure your work to make that happen.

And what is the best way to do so? Research suggests that one effective setup is making a connection to human benefits. You may not be covering a subject that directly involves people, but by packaging it with human relevance, you open readers more quickly to your ideas.

To show how this works, Rachit Dubey and others at Princeton University asked people to read three treatments of a text on the biology of fruit flies. The first treatment listed interesting facts about fruit fly reproduction. The second explained the flies' value to the environment. The third discussed evidence of their value to medical research. Before reading, 200 people rated the value of, and their curiosity about, the assigned reading. After reading, they rated the texts for value and curiosity again.

You can see that the second rating allowed a before/after comparison of curiosity. As you can now guess, people's curiosity hardly budged after reading the list of factoids. It went up a bit after reading the environmental article. It shot up most for the third, about human medicine.[18] The implication for writers applies to all communicators: Package your message to appeal to people's number one concern—themselves. That's what hooks them.

As with surprise and emotion, writing that builds anticipation offers more benefits than just rewarding readers. It helps you get people to remember what you're saying. Psychologist Mathias Gruber and others, in yet another trivia experiment, tested readers' memories for answers. Gruber's team, at the University of California, Davis, first asked questions—"Who was the president of the United States when Uncle Sam first got a beard?" Then they made readers wait 14 seconds for the answers. Like other researchers, they collected ratings of reader curiosity.

A day later, they collected the data they wanted by popping a surprise quiz: How many answers, they asked people, can you remember? Write down all that you're sure of. The readers had viewed 112 questions and answers. They recalled about 71 percent of the answers to questions that had made them very curious (e.g., about Abraham Lincoln), only 54 percent of those that didn't. So the implication was that piquing curiosity is like giving readers a memory enhancer.

The team went further, however. In an interesting twist, in the middle of the 14-second anticipation period, they displayed a picture of a person who had nothing to do with the experiment. The researchers could then answer another question: Would high curiosity for one piece of information (answers to trivia) add to people's ability to recall peripheral information (people pictures) processed at the same time?

And, yes, people recalled 42 percent of the faces when they were curious, 38 percent when they were not. The effect, though small, showed the spinoff benefits of even incidental revving of anticipation.[19] The heightened anticipation creates a memory halo effect. If, like economist Magnani, you piqued readers' curiosity about Titians, Boticellis, and Da Vincis in the Palazzo Strozzi, you would simultaneously make readers better remember everything else you had to say.

THE MAGIC SETUP

You can see the underlying formula for creating anticipation in your writing: Prime, withhold, deliver. As a first step, get readers on the hook. Then tease them with tidbits they can savor. Finally, deliver on your seduction. To elicit rewards, seduce readers with that basic setup. That gets them looking forward to all your great information to come, not to mention heating up suspense by triggering their emotions. Here are five tactics to make that seduction happen.

Promise payoffs. Put up billboards for what's down the road. Tell, then show. Put your message right up front to fuel anticipation for the unveiling of the proof—proof of *how, why,* and *when* your message makes sense.

Wallace Stegner often signaled payoffs when he wrote. Again, in *Beyond the Hundredth Meridian*, as he introduced a nineteenth-century character seizing fame and fortune in the American West: "His career is a demonstration of how far a man could get in a new country on nothing but gall and the gift of gab, so long as what he said was what people wanted to believe...."[20]

You can also signal payoffs with a promise of ideas to come. Here's Stanford neurologist Robert Sapolsky introducing his message in *Behave:* "We don't hate violence. We hate and fear the *wrong* kind of violence, violence in the wrong context. Because violence in the right context is different.... When it's the 'right' type of aggression, we love it."[21]

You'll recognize these sentences as part of topic paragraphs. Your English teachers were right, even if the science wasn't at hand for them to say so: Topic sentences and paragraphs drive a surge of anticipation and even suspense. People can then savor the prospect of examining the evidence that backs up your anticipation-spiking statement.

Recall the old saying about how to construct a good speech: Tell people what you're going to tell them; tell them; and end by telling them what you told them. That's true in part because the formula aids processing fluency. Readers then more easily integrate successive facts into your overall message. But it's also true because it offers the rewards of anticipation.

You can signal payoffs in midstream, too. That signal—more payoffs are on the way!—once again serves as a reward. Here's paleontologist Neil Shubin in the middle of a passage about the evolution of animals: "One of the joys of science is that, on occasion, we see a pattern [in the fossil record] that reveals the order in what initially seems chaotic. A jumble becomes part of a simple plan and you feel you are seeing right through something to find its essence."[22] As a reader, you're enticed to stick with Shubin to later see that essence.

Pique curiosity about things. Make your setup pose a conundrum that you'll unravel. Or invoke mysteries to disclose. Or offer situations that provoke wonder. Make readers alert for cues—predicting, valuing, expecting—as you defer answers.

Here's how Nobelist Daniel Kahneman started a chapter about statistics in *Thinking, Fast and Slow:* "A study of new diagnoses of kidney cancer in the 3,141 counties of the United States reveals a remarkable pattern. The counties in which the incidence of kidney cancer is lowest are mostly rural, sparsely populated, and located in traditionally Republican states in the Midwest, the South, and the West. What do you make of this?"[23]

You can't help but read on—even if you're a statistician who can guess: The kinds of counties in which the incidence is the highest are also those in which the incidence is the lowest because small counties offer small statistical samples with both high and low outliers. On your way to learning that fact, you relish Kahneman's impending resolution of your curiosity.

Questions are hard to beat as setups.[24] David Markowitz, an analytics professor at the University of Oregon, starts an article: "Technology has given people more ways to connect, but has it also given them more opportunities to lie?"[25]

Pique curiosity about people. Your readers are naturally nosy. What weaknesses are dragging down the people you write about? What strengths are driving them forward?

When you tell a story or anecdote—more on that in chapter 8—you'll of course describe people's professed aims, for instance, better town planning. But you'll get more reward mileage if you reveal their hidden agenda, too. What matters to them personally? What are their inner motives? And how will that play out?

If you're writing examples for a manual, of course, skip this tactic. If you're writing anything else, reward readers by slipping motives into the text. Signal to readers that you'll bring closure to the wants and needs of a person. That gets them to anticipate that two-tiered payoff.

Tech consultants Josh Sullivan and Angela Zutavern wrote about the ethics of artificial intelligence by featuring entrepreneur Will Smith, CEO of Euclid Analytics. Along with

Smith's business challenges, they underlined his personal ones. "From the day of the company's launch in 2011 . . . Smith wanted to create an 'enduring' company."[26] That elicited anticipation for knowing how Smith would reconcile both his work and life goals.

Although common sense, perhaps, Helena Alicart and others at the University of Barcelona sought some proof about just how much people get swept up in curiosity about other people. They gave people three 50-question sets of trivia questions about celebrities: one about incidentals, one about "neutral" facts, one about personal gossip, oddities, rumors, and love affairs. A question from the latter: "In, 1987, Tom Cruise had a romance with the singer . . ."

When they measured people's brain waves, the gossip drove the biggest increase in wave activity related to rewards. This is not to suggest that gossip deserves room in your writing, only that surfacing elements of humanness does. People have a thirst for—and anticipate—what makes others tick (Cher, in Tom Cruise's case). They want to know how the sparring goes as people struggle to reconcile the impulses of their lesser and higher selves.

Invent what-ifs. If you don't have juicy material on hand to drive curiosity, invent it. "What would happen if . . . ?" "Imagine that . . ." "Picture yourself when . . ." Manufacture scenarios.

Hypotheticals, of course, routinely fill all our minds, as day in and out we predict and expect all manner of things. We've done so since childhood. What would I do if all my teeth fell out? The technique is as natural as imagining a pillow-popping treasure from the Tooth Fairy, and naturally fuels anticipation.

Here's how Steven Levitt and Stephen Dubner took advantage of a hypothetical to start *Freakonomics:* "Imagine for a moment that you are the manager of a day-care center. You have a clearly stated policy that children are supposed to be picked up by 4 p.m. But very often parents are late. The result: at day's end, you have some anxious children and at least one teacher who must wait around for parents to arrive. What to do?"[27]

Even in serious nonfiction, you have broad license to make things up. Readers don't care so long as you make points and deliver on your promise—and use scenarios that spring from the veracity of your research.

Flash ahead. Foreshadowing and flash-forwarding work not just in literature. Snapshots of what's ahead—of people, plot points, and place names—get readers' anticipation circuits firing. The effect is the same as that produced in movie trailers and vacation planning.

Say you're writing about small business startups. You plan to feature businesspeople in three industries who are acting locally to sell globally. You could start by foreshadowing locales and themes: "The products are in stores around the world. In Paris and Dubai and Shanghai. The makers are in cities that rarely get the spotlight. Tuscaloosa and Bangor and Flagstaff. So what's the secret for a small business in achieving such far-flung distribution?"

You've let your readers know the subject—distribution for small businesses. You've spurred them to predict what goods are made in these small towns. And you've gotten them to anticipate the payoff of stories from those locales. That's a lot to savor. You've got the rewards flowing, even though you're about to write about the nuts and bolts of daily business.

Your readers are like you. They need merely a hint of your upcoming tour stops to imagine—and relish the expectation of—the stops themselves. You might think that too much flashing ahead could dampen curiosity. As a writer, you risk spoiling the payoff, especially the climax.

But science shows that, unless you're writing a mystery or thriller, the risk is overblown. Jonathan Leavitt of the University of California, San Diego, found that people reading stories often enjoyed them *more* when they knew the ending.

Yes, spoilers may spoil the punchline in jokes, but in stories Leavitt showed they don't spoil enjoyment overall. The antici-pation of how events play out winds up our reward circuits aplenty. Leavitt's theory: The early heads-up helps readers better understand—and thus enjoy—your story as it unfolds.[28]

In other words, your readers may know *what* happens but not *how.* That surely helped *Into Thin Air,* John Krakauer's chronicle of a calamitous 1996 Mount Everest expedition, seize readers' reward circuits. Krakauer put the ending right up front. Chapter one, paragraph five: "Later—after six bod-ies had been located, after a search for two others had been abandoned, after surgeons had amputated the gangrenous right hand of my teammate Beck Weathers—people would ask why . . . had climbers on the upper mountain not heeded the signs" of bad weather.[29]

Readers get rewarded by the longer buildup. As Krakauer knew, and Stegner knew, spoilers don't kill the suspense. They may double it. So, immerse readers in the flow of your writing with cues to what's ahead. Preview the direction of your message. Pique curiosity about destinations and motives—stirring the desire *to know*. As readers' anticipation swells, you'll keep them ever on the lookout for the next payoff—another episode in the what, the why, or the how. They will be leaning forward in their seats, even bouncing on their toes.

CHAPTER 6

KEEP IT SMART

For the Love of Readers: Spark Ahas!

Ever stammer mentally to put words to an idea? And then go "Aha!" and warble with delight? Your mind, in a pop, erupts with an insight. It's as if you've flung yourself free from a mental jail. With your eyes in the light, you marvel at the fresh truths now sparkling in the sunshine.

Reproducing that sensation is the next secret to winning over readers. Reward them with the promise—and realization—of leaps of understanding. Give them the blue sky of insight to guide them out of prison. It goes without saying that readers want you to make them feel smarter. Helping them feel that way—repeatedly—engages them with rewards.

Why do smart sayings endure for centuries? Hundreds of years after great writers leave this world, their epigrams and epigraphs resonate. From the 1700s, Samuel Johnson (1709–1784): "Hope is itself a species of happiness, and, perhaps, the chief happiness which this world affords."[1]

From the 1800s, Charlotte Brontë (1816–1855): "Prejudices, it is well known, are most difficult to eradicate from the heart whose soil has never been loosened or fertilized by education: they grow there, firm as weeds among stones."[2]

From the 1900s, James Baldwin (1924–1987): "I imagine that one of the reasons people cling to their hates so stubbornly is because they sense, once hate is gone, that they will be forced to deal with pain."[3]

Baldwin, Brontë, Johnson, giants of their time, carry on an active afterlife. Their words show that writers don't engage just through simplicity, specifics, surprise, emotion, anticipation, and other strategies. They engage by helping readers learn, and especially learn through receipt of the ultimate learning treat: ahas.

Ahas of all varieties. Ahas that give new perspectives, that reveal breakthrough ideas, that restructure tired thinking, that make simple sense from complexity, that integrate, synthesize, and generalize thought. Of course, you can't bowl your readers over with an aha in every paragraph. But you can aspire to deliver more powerful insights—and to amply feed your readers' intellectual hunger.

THE LEARNING CRAVE

The story of research into the effects of learning shows that insights of all kinds reward readers. Even straightforward learning, let alone ahas, rewards people to some extent. A team led by Alex Pine at the University of Haifa in Israel asked people to read a history of the Falkland Islands. The history focused on the war between Argentina and the United Kingdom in 1982. The reading took about 35 minutes. Two days later, the team put everyone in an fMRI machine and quizzed them for 20 minutes on 100 Falkland War facts.

Imagine you were taking the quiz. First you would be asked a question. Example: How many weeks did the war last? You would then be asked to press a button to choose one of four answers (15, 10, 2, or 22 weeks). You would also be asked to rate how confident you were in the answer. Confidence was a proxy measure for how much you would be about to learn (or relearn) about the war. The answer would then flash on a screen. At the moment of the flash, researchers would snap images of your brain's activity.

The research question: What would people find most rewarding during the quiz? The resulting data showed that the bigger the gap between the predicted knowledge and the actual facts, the stronger the reward reaction in their brains. In other words, the more they learned, the more they were rewarded. Moreover, the lower the readers' confidence in answers, the higher the action in their reward circuit when they were right. The higher their confidence, the lower the action in the circuit when they were wrong. In other words, the updating of knowledge, right or wrong, recruited the reward circuit.

Pine's team established a basic fact: The moment when you learn something (or update learning), your brain produces a special response. It hooks directly into your system for valuing rewards and creating pleasure.[4] Learning of even the most basic kind can elicit your motivating impulses. Other research shows that when people learn facts as minor as the definition of a new word, the reward circuit engages.[5]

You can think of the keep-it-smart strategy this way: Readers are yearning for super-knowledge, super-perspective, and super-mastery of ideas. As humans, they are craving thoughts that give them an edge in surviving and thriving. When you play on that impulse, you can spark desire, deliver pleasure, and win them over with engagement.

THE NATURE OF AHAS

Pine's team shows as a start that readers enjoy even nickels and dimes of information. But is small change enough when you're writing to get people to stick with you? Will helping them smarten up with basic facts engage them for long? The research on insight is clear: Gold coins of insight pay better. If you can up the level of insight to ahas, you can help readers hit the reward jackpot. That is the implication of many years of research on insight, and that is the challenge before every writer seeking to firmly engage readers.

Most of the research on insight does not feature experiments with text. Scientists employ other stimuli to allow them to mimic the moment of insight to examine how people respond. One time-tested way scientists favor to study insights is to ask people to read three words and then find a fourth to make a compound out of the first three.[6] For example, consider "house," "bark," and "apple." What fourth word can you find that works to create a compound of all three, that is, that would go before or after, akin to a prefix or suffix?

You can solve word problems of this kind in two ways. One way is analytical, when you test solutions via trial and error. The other is intuitive, when you come up with an answer in a flash of inspiration. Scientists call the arrival of a flash response an "aha moment," the term they use for the purest form of insight. They use EEG signals and fMRI scans to document what then is happening in your brain.

You're probably working on the house-bark-apple problem right now. If you end up solving it via insight, you'll experience a classic brain signal for an aha moment—just as you blurt out the solution, "tree." If you come up with an answer by experimenting, you will exhibit a different, and less rewarding, signal.[7]

Another way scientists study the nature of insight is asking people to solve anagrams. Yongtaek Oh and colleagues at Drexel University asked people to rearrange sets of letters, either a word or nonword, to come up with another word. Example: "Tawer" becomes "water," and "magma," "gamma." Oh's team equipped 30 people with fabric caps fitted with 64 EEG electrodes to run this experiment. Then, with people wired, his team had them read 185 anagrams. People got 16 seconds to view each one. When they had an answer, they pressed a button to report whether it came in a flash of insight or through analysis.

Oh's team knew from earlier research that insight set off a more powerful signal than analysis. So, they took the intensity of the signal recorded during analytic answers—made during conscious, deliberate thought—and subtracted it from the signals during thought disconnected from analysis. Again and again, the resulting insight signal showed a surge of electrical activity for insight in the prefrontal cortex, just over the eye (in the orbitofrontal cortex, or OFC), the value-assessing member of the reward circuit.

They could infer that the moment of insight gives problem solvers an experience of pleasure. That's because the orbitofrontal cortex plays the same valuation role in the reward circuit for experiences like eating, socializing, orgasm, and listening to music. The EEG signal frequency, in the so-called gamma-band, also reflected findings in previous research, which linked that band to people's reaction when getting praise, especially when the praise is unexpected.[8]

LEARNING REWARDS

When you're writing, you're asking readers to perform a process similar to solving word riddles, that is, processing words and language in different ways to comprehend meaning. If you're putting together ideas in especially creative ways, you're also asking them to make foreign or faraway associations, just what happens with the compound-word problems. We can infer that the reward enjoyed by readers from getting an insight from what you say resembles the reward of getting an insight from a word riddle.

Of course, when you're writing, you're raising issues and guiding readers down your chosen path to your chosen aha— an aha you've come to yourself, one that you're sharing. You might presume that holding readers' hands as they read their way to your insight, instead of their finding insights on their own, might ruin the reward signal. One of the salutary effects of aha-like moments, after all, is surprise.

But this is where the research on insight becomes especially instructive for writers. A team led by Jasmin Kizilirmak at the University of Hildesheim in Germany used the three-word format in a novel way to show that people appreciated insights *even if they don't come up with them themselves.* Kizilirmak's team posed 180 riddles for readers and then, after a 6- to 12-second interval, *displayed* the answers. People didn't have enough time to figure them out (example: "cloth," "tennis," "manners"). They had just long enough to wonder about the answers.

In images from the fMRI scanner, the reward circuit still fired handily. The harder the riddle, the greater the firing.[9] People get a strong reward even when you lead them to an insight. They don't have to arrive at it themselves. Kizilirmak's team showed something else—that more than the dopamine-rich midbrain responsible for pleasure came alive at the time of the answer (in this case, "table"). So did the hippocampus and amygdala. That suggests that insights engage readers with reward not just from the insight effect alone but probably from both surprise and emotion.

A host of experimental setups find that valuable learning—ranging from rote learning to moderate insights to ahas—pleases people.[10] At the top end of intensity, however, ahas spur a rush of dopamine not just in the desire-producing parts of the reward circuit but also in the pleasure hotspots fired up by natural opioids. This likely explains why so many people enjoy both work and play that allows them to produce, learn, and indulge in insights—work and play like inventing gadgets, piecing together research findings, doing crossword puzzles, and reading murder mysteries.

Of course, you might be thinking that the most potent insights for readers come not from what you write. They come from readers putting your thinking together with theirs to come to a eureka moment all their own. Many readers experience ahas that way, but you can't control that experience. You can, however, provide a fertile field for those insights to sprout, allowing readers to nurture ahas they never would otherwise have enjoyed.

DIM DELIGHTS

What happens in readers' brains on the way to insight? Scientists infer that the brain is always hungry for insight, just like it's hungry for other stimuli. In search of a new realization, and having no luck running the corridors of conscious thought, it tires of the analytical approach. Without an easy boulevard to realization, it bushwhacks along fainter paths to see what it can find. That's when a pop of insight arrives.

Put another way, the brain is quick to travel pathways to make routine connections. At the same time, though, it doesn't confine itself to those well-worn paths. It tries to make new dim and distant connections. When the search for the dim and distant gets the upper hand during "coarse" processing, the brain works once-disparate material into new wholes. The pop of an aha results.[11]

This is the theory of scientists like Mark Beeman, a pioneer in the neuroscience of insight at Northwestern University. As neurons fire not between established crossroads in the brain but between scattered outposts, a new structure of thought comes to mind. Says Beeman: "It *seems* to happen suddenly, even though it might have been brewing in your head for a while. You wonder, Wow, where did that come from?"

One reason you wonder is that it can come so fast. Oh and his team, using the anagrams as a stimulus, found the pop arrives in a lot less time than an answer that comes during analytically derived solutions, at about 4.5 seconds for insight versus 6 seconds for analytical.[12]

The nature of the restructuring varies. It might be when you see sense in a paradox, re-sequence cause and effect, shed biases to form new views, distill simplicity from complexity, or reinterpret reality in light of new facts. You see another picture, perhaps the big picture, the system-wide picture, the picture behind the picture, or the slap-on-the-forehead picture that was right in front of you the whole time.

As for writers wanting to generate insights to better reward readers, Beeman notes, "The challenge is, how do you look for a weakly activated idea?" He offers an analogy: How do you look for a dim star at night? You can't look directly, because looking directly doesn't allow your eyes, structured the way they are, to see enough light.

"You look from the corner of your eye," he says. The periphery of the eye has more rods for sensing dim light, so by glancing from the side, you can make out what's otherwise barely visible in the night sky. Developing an insight works in the same way. You can't win by focusing on mental activity that's front and center, even as your brain strives to take that approach. Beeman admits: "It's really hard to pay attention with the corner of your mind." But that is the challenge.

Rising to that challenge offers a big payoff, because in the corner of your mind is the source of especially intense ahas. That's where the dim and distant arise. And when they come together, that's when EEG devices recording alpha, or long-wavelength, signals, show a surge moments before the pop, which occurs on the right side of the brain near the right temple—the anterior temporal lobe.[13] That's the initial neural signature of an aha.

Starting 20 years ago, Beeman and John Kounios at Drexel University documented that signature. They also documented that, at the aha moment itself, gamma, or short-wavelength, signals explode.

Research by a Chinese team led by Wangbing Shen and others at Hohai University gives you an idea of the impact. They catalogued emotions that then arose. They found that people solving compound-word problems reported 98 categories of emotions, an average of 16 varieties per person, varying from happiness to surprise. Happiness ranked well above all others (followed by certainty and then calm and excitement).[14]

From this research, you might wonder if scientists could artificially induce that signature and spur insightful thinking. Scientists have had that question, too. A team led by psychologist Carola Salvi and others (including Beeman) asked people to solve compound-word problems while a low electrical current on the scalp excited neurons in the right anterior temporal lobe. Such a current is known to turn on neurons under the skull surface for as long as 90 minutes.

Would action in the right temporal tissue *cause* insightful thinking? The answer appears to be yes. Stimulation of that region increased the percentage of problems people could solve from 39 to 43 percent. The improvement lasted for 20 minutes.[15] Of course, these findings don't offer an aid to writing. But Beeman offers one aid that does come from his research:

To produce insights, get in a positive mood. Although nobody has pinned down the precise mechanism, research shows a positive mood promotes insight production—and your ability to pass the rewards of that insight on to readers.

WRITING TO THINK

The strategy of keeping it smart differs from other writing strategies. To make the most out of it, you have to ruminate with it in mind *before* you write, calling on your intuition and judgment to put the dim and distant together in new ways. You can't drum up most ahas on the run. Ralph Waldo Emerson, always a fountain of insights, said, "You have first an instinct, then an opinion, then a knowledge, as the plant has root, bud and fruit. Trust the instinct to the end, though you can render no reason."[16]

One way to control this maturation to fruit is to divide your writing effort between what I call "writing to think" and "writing to deliver." Commit your thoughts first to a napkin, envelope, or journal. Test faint associations. Connect dimly related concepts. Toy with restructuring your thinking—reorganizing, synthesizing, differentiating, generalizing. Do all this when you're not yet pressed by a deadline. Be patient for the bud to open.

Getting your thinking straight before deadline pressure mounts gives you a big edge. That's not just because you allow yourself more time. Research by Beeman and others shows that insights come faster not only when you're in a good mood but when you're relaxed (one study suggests you watch funny film clips to get that way).[17] You then more easily recognize new patterns, see your issue's hidden roots, re-sequence logic into a new persuasive flow, and devise ways to drive anticipation.

So here's a simple motto: Don't write until you're ready. Let the bud of thought mature first.

As Virginia Woolf is credited with saying, "As for my next book, I am going to hold myself from writing it till I have it impending in me: grown heavy in my mind like a ripe pear; pendant, gravid, asking to be cut or it will fall."[18] When your ideas are ready to fall, then go to the keyboard. You will then be nodding your head with confidence that you've got a valuable realization in hand. You're ready to write to deliver.

Here are five tactics to develop and deliver your best insights. Each one puts you in a position to win over readers and break out with influence.

Challenge convention. Ask readers to join you in re-examining accepted wisdom. By putting convention on trial, by introducing evidence for its flaws, you open readers to adopting new conventions. People will stick with you for the rewards.

Nate Silver in *The Signal and the Noise*: "A Major League shortstop has some plays he can always make, some plays he can never make, and some he'll have to dive for. The diving plays are the most spectacular and will catch our attention. But they lead to a myopic view of the shortstop's abilities."[19]

Silver flips prevailing logic. Some diving catches, he explains, may come not from skilled shortstops but those slow to initially move to the ball. Are diving shortstops better? He spurs you to cast aside a view you might otherwise have held as common sense. You get another view, at first dim and distant, but far more intriguing—and rewarding.

In *Getting to Yes,* Roger Fisher and William Ury guided a generation of readers by challenging the wisdom of the effectiveness of hard-bargaining tactics. Here's one of their challenges to convention: "A lot of time spent in negotiation is spent criticizing. Rather than resist the other side's criticism, invite it."[20]

Of course, your readers don't have to agree with you. But when you find convention wanting, question it in search of a new aha. Bring readers to a once-uncommon—but sound—new structure for thought.

Reframe your message. In the same way as a landscape painter, don't rule out dim, distant, or disparate perspectives. Take an approach that provides a new view that reveals new insight.

Remember that your readers, to make sense of any writing, are going to ask early on: Have I visited this territory? They activate memories to ask, Do I have an on-the-shelf thought pattern to work from to grasp this idea? They're also going to be skeptical and ask, Have I heard this before? Should I pay attention at all? Your intellectual frame, just like your emotional one (chapter 4), shapes not just the insight you give them but the reward.

Legendary CEO Max De Pree, in *Leadership Is an Art,* wrote: "The first responsibility of a leader is to define reality. The last is to say thank you. In between the two, the leader must become a servant and a debtor."[21] De Pree gets you thinking about roles dim and distant from ordinary leadership.

"Servant" and "debtor," as frames, turn rewarding as they coax you to look at De Pree's fresh view of what makes a boss effective.

A frame alone can provoke an insight. Here's Irving Stone in his history of emigrant parties settling the Far West of the United States in the 1800s: "Each emigrant train [including the Donner Party] has an individuality and life cycle comparable to that of a human being: conception, birth, youth, maturity, death, dissolution and immortality."[22]

Stone tells us right off how he will characterize transcontinental emigrant wagon trains in a way you would never have thought of before. Just as important, like De Pree, he provides a structure for delivering further insights later in the text.

Make distinctions. What's the difference between one thing and another when they *appear* the same? Sometimes just dimly lit distinctions. Shine a light on them. Exposing once faintly intertwined threads of an idea can spawn new insights.

In *Ethics for the Real World,* Ronald Howard and Clinton Korver draw distinctions that come from highlighting formerly dimly lit threads. They introduce permutations of the Golden Rule: The platinum rule: "Do unto others as they would have you do unto them." The silver rule: "Do not do unto others as you would not have them do unto you." The brass rule: "Do unto others as they do unto you." Aluminum (cheap imitation) rule: "Do not let others do to you what you would not do to them." And so on.[23] The rules open your eyes to thinking you never experienced before.

Writer Toni Morrison, during her Nobel Prize lecture, opened eyes similarly but with another kind of distinction, in this case about writing: "Oppressive language does more than represent violence; it is violence; does more than represent the limits of knowledge; it limits knowledge."[24]

Invent metaphor. When you're building a house, you can always get the job done with everyday tools and materials. The same goes for building meaning. You can assemble thoughts with common, plain, standard wording. Like a master builder, you get a sturdy product.

But what about when you want to capture nonstandard thought—thought in which standard designs fail to highlight subtleties, fail in curb appeal, fail to turn readers to fans? You can still rely on plain words. Keeping it simple works! But you may do better to tap an alternative: metaphors and figures of speech.

This is the second time I have urged you to use metaphors. I did so in chapter 4, as they offer such big rewards via emotion. I do so here because they offer big rewards via insight. The power of metaphors in engaging readers—and their integral role in writing with impact—obliges me to stress their use doubly. They, working alone, can transform your writing from merely clear to engaging.

Contrary to what you might think, figurative language is not the province of just artists. Or of fiction writers. Experts reckon that people use 50 metaphors per 1,000 words in formal communication. That can add up to millions in a 60-year life span.[25] You no doubt use them much more than you think. Your facility with them stems from learning nearly everything about both thoughts and objects in association with some tangible context as a kid—"racing like the devil" to get to school on time.

Researcher Serena Mon and colleagues quantified how well just simple metaphors engage readers. They used a device that measures pupil dilation, a gauge of attention and arousal. They compared reader responses to, for example, "The matter was *out of the editor's hands* after she sent the text" with "The matter was *out of the editor's control* . . ." The first one, though using familiar metaphor, dilated pupils more than the second, which used a literal substitute.[26]

To create an insight, of course, you have to be much more creative in capturing reader attention than using simple and common metaphors. As a start, consider how science writer Carl Zimmer, profiling failed scientist John Butler Burke, noted how Burke was hounded by reporters during an initial success: "Burke at first shied away from claiming too much for his [faulty] discovery. But they gnawed at his resolve like termites in old wood."[27]

That's a metaphor to capture a small insight about one element of a man's personality. But you can use metaphor just as well to capture big insights to frame an entire book. Here's what Thomas Friedman did: "Columbus reported to his king and queen that the world was round, and he went down in history as the man who first made this discovery. I returned home [from a reporting trip in India] and shared my discovery only with my wife, and only in a whisper. 'Honey,' I confided, 'I think the world is flat.'"[28]

Of course, if you were writing a book about globalization, you could say, "In recent years, the world has gotten a lot closer and connected." But you can see how the metaphor offers a unique way of delivering not just the message but a timeless insight.

Surface truths. For every practical truth, there's often a parallel universal one. If what you say is true in business, is it true in the community? If it's true in politics, is it true in the family? We all live multiple lives. What truths cut across them? Connections on the surface may seem dim and distant. But when you reveal the commonality underneath, they can reward readers with an aha.

Max De Pree on leadership. Irving Stone on emigration. Ronald Howard and Clinton Korver on the Golden Rule. These authors engage readers not just from insights about their topic, but by broaching, in parallel or figuratively, perennial truths. When you're writing to get ready, explore how you can expand your thinking in the microcosm of your subject to resonate in the macrocosm of people's experience.

John Butman shows how simple this can be in his book about developing breakthrough ideas in business. One of his sentences: "If you do not fascinate yourself, you cannot fascinate others."[29] His message was meant to apply to fascinating yourself with an idea relevant to your profession, but it could apply just as much to friendships and raising kids. He didn't even have to say so. Just by the way he composed his idea, he opened readers to that aha.

One way to do this is to test the way you phrase your messages, by analogy, to see if they work broadly.[30] You can have fun at the same time. Here's Helen Czerski writing about physics in *Storm in a Teacup:* "Last night, I did a bit of ballistic cooking and made popcorn. It's always a relief to discover that a tough, unwelcoming exterior can conceal a softer inside . . ."[31] She crafts an everyday insight but it balloons into a universal one.

When you build smarts like that into your writing, you deliver more than information and explanation. You engage readers' minds at a loftier intellectual level. The dim and distant combined spark new, rewarding wholes. You're not going to fling readers free of a mental jail in every sentence, but you can spark more flashes of light by regularly reminding yourself: Everyone loves a good aha.

CHAPTER 7

KEEP IT SOCIAL

For the Love of Readers: Connect!

How do you express yourself when only your dog is listening? That hints at the seventh secret to engaging readers. Reveal yourself. Give readers clues as to what's going on in your head. Let them connect with you, the author, as a thinking and feeling person.

People, and readers, have an inference engine. They infer your personality, beliefs, and motives from your display of voice, worldview, vocabulary, wit, syntax, poetic rhythm, sensibilities, and much more. They do the same for the people you write about.

Readers wake instantly to a chance to connect with you. They also want to connect with the people you include in stories and examples. They, like you, crave to know the intellectual and emotional life of those they're associating with. And they are rewarded when they can make that connection.

There's nothing more human than that. Hardwiring prods us to take the measure of other people. How else to assure the well-being of ourselves, our family, our tribe? How else to advance ourselves among our fellows? "At baseline, human beings are social animals, and we're drawn to social things," says psychologist David Dodell-Feder at the University of Rochester. "We as a species have this fundamental interest in social things that outpaces our interest in non-social things."[1]

We are particularly eager, as scientists like Dodell-Feder say, to "mentalize," or more simply, to mind-read, to suss out what's in other people's heads. Writers can't re-create the rich effect of interacting with people face-to-face, but they can do something almost as potent. They can drive mind-reading: Through examples, anecdotes, what-if scenarios, and stories, writers can get readers to impulsively glean what's in their minds and in the minds of people in their writing.

As a test, to show how much of an impact this has, here's Lewis Thomas again in *Lives of a Cell*. See if you can resist the impulse to glean what's going on in his mind as he fancies what kind of music would best explain humans to extraterrestrials: "I would vote for Bach, all of Bach, streamed out into space, over and over again. We would be bragging, of course, but it is surely excusable for us to put the best possible face on at the beginning of such an acquaintance."[2]

Thomas surely won the National Book Award at least in part because he wrote to allow, indeed prompt, readers to think about what he and the people he was writing about were thinking. And that mind-to-mind connection is an element of social connection that you can accentuate to engage readers. When you help readers relate to you and the people on your writing stage, you help them connect as if in person. From that the rewards flow.

To be sure, if you're a reporter for the local news, making a social connection as the author of an article may not be appropriate. As a journalist, I was instructed to keep myself and my dog out of the picture. That's a rule of the trade. In news stories, the writer must be kept invisible. Readers shouldn't care a whit about you. Let alone your dog.

But if you're writing for general readers, you'll win people over if you remember everyone is, at the core, a social hound. We keep our noses to the ground for signs of humanity. Readers thirst for clues to who you are, what matters to you, how you feel, and what you intend. Would you vote to stream Bach, too? How do you speak to your dog, anyway?

Readers can't help but theorize what's going on in your mind. This may mean you engage readers best by revealing yourself subtly, as I often do in this book. Or it may mean pouring out your sensibilities—as Thomas did—"over and over again." Finding the right balance might take experimentation. But on your first draft, don't worry about overdoing it. Remember, only your dog is listening.

As legendary essayist E. B. White says in *The Elements of Style,* all writing "is communication through revelation—it is the Self escaping into the open."[3] Let people (and your dog) see enough of you in the open to speculate on your thoughts and feelings. Let them do the same for the people you write about. They'll feel rewarded by both. You can always edit out any overwriting and silly talk when you rewrite.

SOCIAL OBSESSION

People's drive to infer other people's thoughts, desires, intentions, and emotions rivals every other human drive, and for good reasons. As social animals, getting a fix on others, deciding whom to trust, whom to partner with, whom to ask for help, whom to learn from—that all underpins our survival. As much today as millennia ago, our success in work and life depends on it.[4]

So we all pursue social cues, forever busy decoding people's mental states, whether in person or when reading a text.[5] We want to know so much about those around us: What are they thinking about us? What are they thinking we're thinking about them? What are they thinking others are thinking about them? And so on. We also want to know what others are feeling.[6]

We're then poised to adjust our behavior. What will he or she do next—and how will I react? What will he or she say—and how should I reply? Detecting, inferring, speculating—this mental theorizing, this mind-reading, is a core mental process.[7] A more scientific term for it is "theory of mind." Theorizing about what's in others' minds is an always-on mental operation.

Our minds can't help but interrogate every stimulus for social meaning. Ever seen a face in your toast? Or in the clouds? That's not just your healthy imagination. It's your hardwired drive to detect social information in everything from what's in front of you to what's in the blue sky above.[8] Your brain even processes social signals through specialized pathways,[9] which scientists have documented by testing people with everything from pictures of faces to receipt of praise from others.[10]

When it comes to understanding the extent of mind-reading during reading, scientists have tested people reading texts that vary from plain expository pieces to stories to poetry. In every instance, readers' brains fire up in the same regions.

A patch of gray matter called the temporoparietal junction, or TPJ, figures prominently in the action.[11] Just above and behind your ears, the TPJ is not the only brain region that gets in the act. A larger network of mind-reading regions does.[12] But the TPJ serves as a mind-reading, or theory-of-mind, hub.[13]

Of course, a lot of writing about people and situations has social content—description of someone's T-shirt or hair color, for instance. Research shows that the implied presence of others through such detail does enliven our social circuits. But studies show that when people encounter social cues that don't prompt mind-reading, the effect on the TPJ is muted. It stays largely silent.[14] Readers still make predictions, but they don't get hooked by the richer mind-reading experience.

Ironically, driven as we are to mind-read, we're not that good at getting our inferences right. Research shows that people accurately infer only about 20 percent of how strangers are feeling. The percentage is 30 percent for close friends. We max out at 35 percent or so for spouses.[15] We're not psychics. Still, we desperately wish we were. We're driven to keep trying, thirsty for clues that give us any useful material.

How does the power of the keep-it-social strategy compare to that of the other seven strategies? How much reward does it give? When will a reader feel more rewarded when you "keep it social" versus "keep it smart"? Scientists don't have a clear answer. The question raises the age-old challenge of comparing apples and oranges. How do all those neurons weigh the reward of one kind of writing compared to another?

Scientists can point to a simple mechanism for how we derive the answer: The brain, like a global money changer at the airport, converts the assessed value of all promised rewards into what researchers call a "common currency."[16] The prefrontal cortex, firing during the reward circuit, does this job. It's as if the sharp-eyed money changer translates everything that's on the reward table into dollars or euros.

That then allows the mind to weigh options that originally compared poorly. It trades off their value easily now that they're in common terms, and in a snap decision, makes a choice. This calculation goes on all the time in your mind. Your brain is even now deciding whether to continue reading this book. Would another book on, say, Italian cooking, yield more value? And how does that compare to going out for a drink at Starbucks?

How you as a writer make that trade-off—going with specifics, surprise, seduction, smarts, or any combination—is not something science can teach you. That brings you to the threshold where the science ends and the art begins. When you sit down to write, you have to make the choice with intuition. When it comes to the keep-it-social strategy, though, take your cue from Lewis Thomas. When you connect with readers by revealing yourself in your work, you put an engaging expression on the otherwise characterless face.

SOCIAL TRIGGERS

One challenge for neuroscientists in gauging the power of mind-reading has been isolating its effect from effects driven by other social factors. Hundreds of experiments in recent years, however, have been able to confirm a consistent pattern in the TPJ and related regions.[17] The trick used by many experimenters has been to ask people to read so-called false-belief stories. False-belief stories feature characters whose thinking, owing to a sudden turn of events, contradicts reality. If you're the one reading one of the stories, you're forced to wonder: What could that person in the story have been thinking?

In an early experiment, Rebecca Saxe and others at MIT asked people to read stories like this one: "A boy is making a papier-mâché project for his art class. He spends hours ripping newspaper into even strips. Then he goes out to buy flour. His mother comes home and throws all the newspaper strips away."

You're going to wonder a couple of things after reading this story: What was going on in the mind of the mother who had a "false belief"? And of course, what would happen in the boy's mind when he got back from the store?

For comparison, Saxe's team also asked the same people to read stories like this one, without a person in it: "A pot of water was left on low heat yesterday in case anybody wanted tea. The pot stayed on the heat all night. Nobody did drink tea, but this morning, the water was gone."

Saxe and her team not only compared the mind-reading stimulated by these two stories but also stories falling in between, those with a character in action but not one whose thinking you would necessarily be prompted to infer: "Jane is walking to work this morning through a very industrial area. In one place the crane is taking up the whole sidewalk. To get to her building, she has to take a detour."

The result was that the TPJ on both the left and rights sides of the brain lit up for the false-belief stories. The middle of the

prefrontal cortex did, too. That stemmed from readers making mind-reading inferences—in this case about the thinking
by the mother, the boy, and Jane. The reverse happened for
the other stories, like those about the pot of water without a
human character. In the false-belief stories, the mind-reading
brain was racing; in the others, it idled.

To confirm that mind-reading, not just the presence of
a person, drove so much mental activity, they ran a second
experiment. This time they asked people to read stories that
described just a person's physical detail, such as Jane's height.
Again, although some parts of the social circuits fired, there
was no action in the TPJ.[18] The takeaway? You can get readers
to engage in mind-reading most deeply when they see action
(taking a detour, playing Bach).

Just how deeply do readers inquire into other people's
minds? A number of experiments have shown that when people read a favorite author, or a favorite article with a success
story about an entrepreneur, lawyer, or engineer, they wonder
about that person's goals and traits. A team led by Frank Van
Overwalle at the Vrije Universiteit Brussel (Free University
of Brussels) demonstrated the degree of inferencing by using
"false-recognition" statements.

The team's procedure was to display on a screen a short
statement that implied, in some cases, a person's goals, and in
other cases, traits. After four seconds, they displayed a word
that matched the implied goal or trait in one out of six tests.
When readers received this test word, or probe, they had to
make a snap decision: Was the probe word embedded in the
statements that just flashed by? Hit the "yes" or "no" button.

The team, of course, was forcing readers to answer by reflex, before they could mentally check their results. This revealed whether readers had spontaneously inferred the characters' mental states. Did they establish an inference even though the inference word, a goal or trait, never appeared? Earlier experiments had shown that people, if they encoded strong inferences, would hit the "yes" button even when they were wrong, that is, when they should have hit "no."

To see how this worked, here's one of the statements implying a goal: "He ran with a growling stomach to the bakery." Readers had four seconds to read it. They then got 350 milliseconds to press the "yes" or "no" button once the probe came up—"to eat." Imagine you were a reader. Which button would you press if you had just one-third of a second? The right answer is obviously "no." "To eat" did not appear in the statement. But one-third of people hit "yes," having inferred that the bakery-bound man had a goal of eating.

People had engaged in mind-reading a person's goal without the text saying so. The team found the same thing happened when readers responded to trait statements. Here's one: "Karl stepped on the toes of his girlfriend during the foxtrot." Imagine again that you're the reader. After that statement, the screen goes blank and then flashes "clumsy." Which button would you hit? Again, the correct button is clearly "no." "Clumsy" does not appear in the statement. But forced into a snap answer, in this case in 650 milliseconds, about 25 percent of people hit "yes."

How intensively do people infer? Van Overwalle and his team went a step further to get an idea. They displayed sentences that combined implied goals *and* traits. An example: "The girl turned red when she stood in front of the class with her papers." They then flashed the probe words: "to give a talk" and "shy."[19] And they got the same results. Readers jumped into mind-reading about *both* factors as they were reading.

Van Overwalle and his team knew in advance, from other work, that people infer goals faster than traits.[20] That explains the two different test deadlines, 350 versus 650 milliseconds. You can see how this reflects natural selection. Knowing what people are likely to do, even before knowing what they're like, promotes winning a competition over food, drink, mates, shelter, or anything else a thousand generations ago. Super-fast inferencing of another person's intentions helps us in just the same ways today.

The Van Overwalle team's work raises another question. Do the results of experiments with short bits of text hold up when people are reading longer texts that don't mention people? Does the social inferencing engine get fired up anyway? Nir Jacoby at Columbia University and Evelina Fedorenko at Harvard Medical School asked people to read longer excerpts, around 75 words.

Here's an excerpt of one of their texts: "Lake Baikal is a rift lake in the south of the Russian region of Siberia. It is the largest (by volume) freshwater lake in the world ... home to more than 1,700 species of plants and animals ..." and so on. They found that the longer text did stir action in some regions activated by mind-reading, among them the prefrontal cortex. But it still did not stir mind-reading's telltale patch of tissue, the TPJ.[21]

The accumulation of research prompted Jorie Koster-Hale and Rebecca Saxe at MIT to write, "the presence of a human character in the stimuli is not sufficient: stories that describe a character's physical appearance, or even their internal (but not mental) experiences, like hunger or queasiness or physical pain, elicit much less response than stories about the character's beliefs, desires, and emotions."[22]

You can start to see the outlines of what this science means for tactics to write better. You have a choice as to how to focus your readers' mental processing. Triggering mind-reading has a potent effect on readers' brains. Revealing goals and traits, as a start, just hints at the larger menu of items people infer. Inferencing likely extends to values, motivations, passions, biases, worries, and more. You as a writer partly control these factors and, in turn, the rewards you deliver to readers.

PERSONAL POWER

Outside the fields of neuroscience and psychology, experts have explored the power of social cues in markedly different experimental ways. Researchers in education have explored so-called personalization in writing: communicating in a way to take advantage of the author's implied presence to engage readers. From what we know of neuroscience, we can presume the rewards from personalization stem at least in part, if not all, from the mind-reading effect.

An experiment reported in 2002 by Richard Paxton at the University of Wisconsin shows how this works. He asked a group of Seattle high school sophomores and juniors to read about the murder of Julius Caesar. He had students first read a textbook passage, which detailed Caesar's demise at the hands of Roman senators. The students also read six historical documents. After that prep, each student wrote an essay from what they learned.

Paxton divided the students into two groups. One read the original text, written in the third person (he/they). It revealed little of the presence or thinking of the author, the standard approach in textbooks. The other group read a passage Paxton had edited to use the first person, the author speaking directly to the reader. The edits, though modest, revealed the author's personal beliefs and featured opinion-suggesting phrases like "without a doubt," "unfortunately," and "as you might well imagine."

Paxton uncovered a pattern when he sat with some of the readers and asked them, as part of the experiment, to "think out loud" with their impressions. When he tallied the results, he found that the students in the original-text group referred to the author 28 times compared to 91 times in the modified-text group. These students talked back to the author fewer times and made half as many comments and judgments. In effect, although the students in the original-text group read the same information as the modified group, they absorbed it in different ways. Paxton noted that they just "browsed" for key facts.

The difference was just as striking when it came time for the students to write their essays. The modified-text group wrote 34 percent more. Their writing showed a stronger sense of belief in themselves and their opinions. Instead of browsing, they, in effect, interacted with the author.[23] We can speculate, without fMRI or EEG evidence to confirm it, that the

modified-text group had engaged more in mind-reading—
and in turn enjoyed the motivational effect of the desire and
pleasure produced by the reward circuit.

Other studies reveal similar advantages with personalizing
information for students. Though results vary, some studies
show it improves retention for the text. It may also boost
motivation to read, and as in Paxton's experiment, bolster
students' ability to apply what they learn. This effect appears
to benefit even people listening to computer-training scripts,
when a computer speaks using "I" and "you" instead of delivering a third-person monologue.[24]

Research outside education shows that this effect extends to adults in healthcare. Richard Mayer and others at
the University of California had people view an online presentation on how the respiratory system works. A 100-word
spoken text was accompanied by simple animations of the
lungs and windpipe. The script outlined three steps, inhaling,
oxygen exchange, and exhalation.

The team created two versions, one an impersonal script,
the other with "the" replaced 12 times with "your." They
changed nothing else. A fragment to give you an idea: "During inhaling, the [your] diaphragm moves down, creating
more space for the [your] lungs, air enters through the [your]
nose or mouth, moves down through the [your] throat and
bronchial tubes to tiny air sacs in the [your] lungs . . ."

Echoing Paxton's results, the people who listened to the
personalized version scored significantly higher when tested
on applying what they had learned. The testing included five
questions. One of them: "Suppose you are a scientist trying
to improve the human respiratory system. How could you

get more oxygen into the bloodstream faster?" The "your" group—which, again, heard the same script—gave much better answers. Acceptable ones, for example, included the creation of larger air sacs or a more permeable bloodstream.[25]

As with other writing strategies, the research shows that even the simplest social cues can win readers over. The readers will recognize these cues without thinking, and owing to the brain's hardwiring, enjoy the neurochemical cocktail produced in the reward circuit. People don't want you to quiet the mind-reading in their heads. They want you to turn it on.

GETTING SOCIAL

Aristotle said that persuasion rested on three principles: logos (logic), pathos (emotion), and ethos (the author). This chapter, in effect, is about ethos, the ethos about you, the author, and the ethos of the people you write about. How do you (and others in your writing) think, what do you (and others) value, and how much do you (and others) care?

If readers are to trust you, if they are to believe you have the command of your subject to convey your message, you engage them by opening a window on who you are.

Another way of saying this is that your readers want to get a grip on your character. Are you worth listening to? Are you trustworthy? Do you show confidence in what you're saying? Are you an authority? Are you writing to serve them or serve yourself? Do you have a hidden agenda? Should they stick with your thoughts or dismiss them? And what about the people you're writing about? Do they stand up to standards of authenticity that make them worth believing in and learning from?

Albrecht Küfner and a team at Johannes Gutenberg University Mainz did an experiment that hints at how astute readers are in asking these questions. They wondered just how much of the "big five" personality traits readers inferred from the text of authors. The five traits: neuroticism, extraversion, openness, agreeableness, and conscientiousness. To answer their question, they asked 79 people to spend seven minutes writing fictional stories that included the words "plane crash," "parlor maid," "fireworks," "Middle Ages," and "supermarket." The authors wrote stories varying in length from 32 to 177 words.

They then had observers rate the five big traits revealed by the authors, whose traits had been previously measured during an independent writing task. They also had the observers give their impression of the authors' "general knowledge." The results were mixed but eye-opening. The observers didn't get the neuroticism, extraversion, and conscientiousness ratings right. But they correctly judged openness, agreeableness, and general knowledge. They also agreed with each other on their ratings. And their ratings stemmed solely from judging "linguistic style."

Much more than you thought, readers can infer just from your writing style key elements of your personality. As Küfner and his team wrote, noting that the writing styles were markedly different, one author to another, "Writing and personality go hand in hand. Independent of whether the author is writing a novel, a diary, a . . . message or a blog, word use seems to be linked to the author's cognitive, emotional, and social processes."[26]

We now know just how right E. B. White was in referring to the writer's self "escaping into the open." Even if you're not trying, you inadvertently feed readers clues to prompt accurate judgments during their mind-reading. Küfner's team was assessing fiction, with people forced to write creatively. But we can guess that some of the effect carries over to nonfiction.

With this research in mind, you can now see better how to harness your readers' mind-reading impulse. To start, allow readers to see into your head by cracking your privacy window during composition. Expose yourself and the people you write about. Be transparent in ways you haven't previously. Build your ethos with authenticity readers can see, feel, and trust. Here are tactics for making that happen.

Unearth beliefs, intentions. Make your inner life—and the life of the people you write about—detectable. Don't numb readers' thirst for human connection by using purposefully dry discourse.

Even if your profession calls on you to write stodgy prose, you can find a modest way to spur mind-reading. Put people in your text for starters. As an example, take a sentence that might appear in a brokerage brochure: "Portfolio diversification into international stocks is a good way to buffer investment losses during U.S. downturns." How about this alternative: "When the people we advise get concerned about losing money, we tell them to hedge their bets by buying stocks internationally."

Stories, the subject of the next chapter, make easy entrées to mind-reading. Materials scientist Mark Miodownik started a passage on steel: "As I stood on a train bleeding from what would later be classified as a thirteen-centimeter stab wound, I wondered what to do. It was May 1985, and I had just jumped on to a London Tube train as the door closed, shutting out my attacker, but not before he had slashed my back . . . [with a steel razor]."[27]

Joshua Becker wrote in *Things That Matter*: "Bronnie Ware, an Australian nurse who spent several years caring for people during the last weeks of their lives, routinely asked her patients about any regrets they had or anything they would do differently if they could. Later she posted an article . . . [and] wrote of the phenomenal clarity of vision that people gained at the end of their lives. . . ."[28]

People connect with people. (Remember the fruit fly.) So, give readers not just another word to read but another mind. Don't anesthetize them with anonymity.

Show vulnerabilities. Do you have a weak side? Do the people you write about have one? Unless you're writing news or academic papers, expose your soft spots and those of the people you write about. Put humanity in what you say.

Here's how one pro does it. Hope Jahren writes in *Lab Girl,* "My lab is a place where my guilt over what I haven't done is supplanted by all the things that I am getting done. My uncalled parents, unpaid credit cards, unwashed dishes, and unshaved legs pale in comparison to the noble breakthrough under pursuit. . . ."[29]

Benjamin Bergen, the professor at the University of California, San Diego (chapter 2), starts a chapter in *Louder Than Words,* "If you're like me, your victories in arm wrestling are few and far between, except against the young, the infirm, or the unconscious. [But] . . . if this failing causes you mental anguish, fear not. It turns out that being built like Popeye is not the only way to get the upper hand. . . ."[30]

You can make this work even with simple how-to writings. Say you're writing about skills for charitable fundraising. You could tick off each one, like persuasion, emotional intelligence, and storytelling. But what if you hooked readers by starting with the vulnerability of an expert: "Jake Veranda, a champion fundraiser for the Red Cross, admits that the one thing he dreads is the moment he has to 'make the ask.'"

I made that one up. But in an instant, your empathy spiked. You got connected to the subject on a whole new level. You were mind-reading Jake's feelings, a person who doesn't even exist.

Display voice. How do you best address your audience? As if from a dais? With a hardhat on? From a fireside rocking chair? Choose formal, choose casual, choose offbeat, but choose a style genuine for you.

Business professor Richard D'Aveni writes about the slide of American world leadership: "The veteran U.S. boxer has lost control of the ring and the momentum of the match. In some ways, the United States has been pursuing a rope-a-dope economic strategy, absorbing body blows . . . and waiting for the Chinese challenger to tire. . . ."[31]

This rope-a-dope image, so clearly revealing how D'Aveni thinks, also highlights one writing tactic that deserves yet a third mention: metaphor. Metaphors stir mind-reading because they expose how the writer's mind works figuratively. We can guess that D'Aveni knew, and maybe even admired, the boxing strategy popularized by Muhammad Ali in the 1970s.

To confirm the nature of the mind-reading response that metaphors prompt, Andrea Bowes and Albert Katz at the University of Western Ontario tested how putting them at the end of stories changed people's ability to infer mental states. They asked people to read pairs of identical stories, except one ended with a literal sentence and the other a metaphor.

Here's an example: "Frank knew that Edward wasn't reliable. Frank had told him some personal information and Edward told the rest of their friends about it. Edward suggested that Frank was prone to problems. Frank warned Kyle: Be careful what you say to him [or, alternatively] Watch your back around him."

On a five-point scale, readers rated the people in the metaphor-ending story as being much closer friends, and they also rated their experience as more emotionally intense. The metaphors, concluded Bowes and Katz, telegraphed to readers a social intimacy between characters. They speculated that shared worldly knowledge enabled the mind-reading and in turn human connection.[32]

Invite conversation. Devise passages to get readers interacting with you. Mock up a dialogue, for example, or at least the start of one.

Professor and author Dan Ariely begins a passage on human decision-making: "Have you ever grabbed for a coupon offering a FREE! package of coffee beans—even though you don't drink coffee and don't even have a machine with which to brew it?"[33]

Avinash Dixit and Barry Nalebuff start a passage on strat-egy:"Believe it or not, we are going to ask you to play a game against us. We've picked a number between 1 and 100, and your goal is to guess the number. If you guess correctly on the first try, we'll pay you $100. . . ."

"Are you ready to play?" they ask after explaining the rules. "We are, too." And they draw you into a silent, one-on-one tutoring session.[34] It's an imitation of the real thing, to be sure. But it sparks a round of mind-reading that's not a bad stand-in for being in the classroom with the authors.

Trust "you." Instead of relying on the third person (he/she/they), try "you" to replace "the" or "they." As personaliza-tion experiments show, you'll drive social cognition, which even if not triggering mind-reading, gets processed with reward.

One benefit of using "you" is that it simulates action from the reader's perspective. Instead of observing the action, you encourage readers to participate in it. The way I've been writ-ing this book is an example. I want to maneuver you into joining me in a seat in front of a screen as a writer instead of just watching me blather from the balcony.[35]

Biologist Janine Benyus shows how one pro gets the reader participating: "Think of yourself as a plant, rooted in place, unable to switch your tail or twitch your flanks. You are the succulent object of desire for countless microbes, insects, and animals that can't photosynthesize their own food. You may parry their attacks with leathery leaves, thorns, or perhaps burrowing nettles, but your warfare of choice is chemical."[36]

Experience shows that converting third-person explana-tory text to the second person gives you a further advantage:

You force yourself to adopt a more familiar tone. That tone can encourage you to make your sentences more direct. More direct sentences in turn allow you to slash the word count. A slashed word count drives up processing fluency. You create a virtuous cycle—and a twofer: You get the benefit of keeping it both social *and* simple.

I can't overstate how much triggering mind-reading pleases readers, even if you've never heard of this psychological effect. People want to hear the echoes of what you've been saying to your dog. They want to see into the heart of your characters like Jake Veranda. They yearn for you to illuminate the threads of social connection. Your impact and influence as a writer come not from shutting readers out of mental interiors but from shining a light on the fabric within.

CHAPTER 8

KEEP IT STORY-DRIVEN

For the Love of Readers: Charm with Narrative

Make sure Jane is in trouble. That's the eighth, and perhaps most potent, secret to winning over readers. Reward them with stories about someone struggling. Put them in the saddle of the action, and as the story gallops along, they will hold on tight—and revel in the ride.

Research with fMRI scanners shows just how securely a story holds readers. When you begin, even in the first few lines, you fire up a broad grid of readers' brain circuitry. That circuitry, and its neuronal fibers, extends in many directions. It links to circuits for emotion, social connection, anticipation, and other processing.

What's more, the grid of brain circuitry among readers matches your grid in composing the story. You as writer, your audience as readers—the scans of both of your brains mirror each other. You and your readers undergo what scientists like Uri Hasson at Princeton call a coupling.

This coupling presumably helps explain why the keep-it-story-driven strategy ranks among the most celebrated of all writing strategies. From the moment you open a story as a writer—when you put a protagonist in front of a challenge—you sync a broad swath of your mind's neural activity with that of your audience. Your story entrains readers' brains.

Happy stories and sad stories—it doesn't matter. The engaging effect is universal. You don't have to try to spark this response. It happens innately. Your readers have experienced it since they were toddlers. Research shows that children start telling stories between the ages of three and five, at the same time they learn common story concepts, pretending, grasping false beliefs, and understanding moral blame.[1]

"When it comes to children," says Raymond Mar, a psychology professor and story expert at York University in Toronto, "you do not have to teach children to become interested in stories. They just pop out that way. They're fascinated by stories from the get-go. Developing a fascination for exposition—that comes a bit later, or sometimes not at all."[2]

The draw of stories affects the entire human race. It doesn't matter who your parents were, what country you grew up in, or what cultural traditions you followed. You get sucked into stories naturally, and you tell them naturally, too. Researchers have found them in ancient Sanskrit, Latin, Greek, Chinese, Egyptian, and Sumerian.[3] They're as old as antiquity—emerging more than 30,000 years ago.[4] No culture "invented" them.

You can communicate with impact with stories simply because people have such a hardwired facility for handling them. Stories somehow seem to get a special neural welcome. People also feel rewarded by them, and in whatever context:

in anecdotes and what-if scenarios, success stories and corporate histories, court cases and process-failure reports, essays
and marketing brochures.

That's not to say that logical argument, so common in
workaday writing, doesn't communicate with power. That's
especially true when you take advantage of the other seven
writing strategies. Persuading readers of your convictions
based on propositions and evidence still has plenty of draw.
"There are things exposition can do that narrative cannot,"
Mar notes. "Exposition is absolutely essential for conveying
abstract concepts." He points to many kinds of scientific writing in his own field.

But research shows that argument, or persuasion with the
facts, engages different parts of the brain—traditional control
and language areas.[5] And those parts simply don't, in turn,
engage as many reward-circuit hot buttons. That's of course
why so many pros spend endless hours finding story snippets
to illustrate and communicate their points. They know that
stories spike people's desire and lead to unparalleled reward.

You don't have to use even full stories to deliver their
attention-grabbing effect. Entrepreneur Michael Ventura
opens his book on empathy in business: "'If you don't get
into trouble, you'll never learn how to get out of it.' That was
the advice a friend's dad gave me back in 2003. I was twenty-
three years old, had a little less than two years of advertising
experience, and had just lost my job."[6]

The anecdote doesn't convey Ventura's message. But it
hooks your story circuits on the way to his getting to the
message. He puts you instantly in the saddle. Your neural firing
pattern all at once matched his. He could have simply stated

his message, hooking you with his reasoning. But his use of story entrained more of your brain, initiating a performance of mental processing unique to narrative.

As much as a story snippet can engage readers, of course, longer stories can engage them even more. To demonstrate how that happens in your own mind, I'm going to quote a number of excerpts of a classic of American nonfiction. The writer was a nurse working in a war hospital, tending to a wounded soldier. She first sets the scene of the struggle:

> His mind had suffered more than his body; some string of that delicate machine was over strained, and, for days, he had been reliving in imagination the scenes he could not forget till his distress broke out in incoherent ravings. . . . He lay cheering his comrades on, hurrying them back, then counting them as they fell around him, often clutching my arm, to drag me from the vicinity of a bursting shell, or covering up his head to screen himself from a shower of shot . . .

The story begins to get its grip on you. You can almost feel it. Chemically, that's the effect of dopamine flowing in your brain and, as you enjoy the story, the effect of natural opioids released in response. You can also feel the effect of other writing strategies—keeping it specific, surprising, stirring, social, and so on. And that's why stories engage on many levels: They reward readers at the same time with some or all of the other seven writing strategies.

That's in large part why this story became a runaway classic. The passage setting the scene goes on:

His face [was] brilliant with fever; his eyes restless; his
head never still; every muscle strained and rigid; while
an incessant stream of defiant shouts, whispered warn-
ings, and broken laments poured from his lips with that
forceful bewilderment which makes such wanderings so
hard to overhear.

The story is from *Hospital Sketches* by Louisa May Alcott.
Alcott was then a Civil War nurse, her charges, wounded and
feverish men. In her writing, she was doing what all story
writers before and since have learned they must do first to
engage: Create a setup, a focus on a struggle. In Alcott's case,
the struggle was her heart-wrenching vigil with a Virginia
blacksmith, John.

THE STORY OF STORY

I'll come back to Alcott. But first here's the keystone question by scientists: What in our brains accounts for people's
unusually strong response to stories? Why are we wired so
extensively to comprehend them? Why would nature have
favored a massive neural processing machine to gobble them
up so avidly—and easily? Why do they give writers so much
power to reel in their audiences and communicate with
impact?

Scientists offer many theories about why, over millennia,
stories have become ingrained in the human faculty. One is
that stories offer a means to make sense of otherwise incoherent
experiences.[7] Life as we live it sometimes lacks reason. Why did
we have a drought this year and not last? Where did that new

disease come from? Why did ravens attack the mail carrier? How do you make sense of the death of a Virginia blacksmith? Natural selection favored brains adept at processing stories to allow us to link cause and effect to make life appear coherent.

Another explanation for our highly evolved faculty for stories is their value for training. They give us a way to rehearse actions in our heads before doing them in real life. Keith Oatley, a pioneer in story research, likens this to practicing on an internal flight simulator.[8] With a simulator, you invent scenarios to master and run thought experiments to test yourself. The session in the simulator can later prove face-saving, if not lifesaving, because you gain new reasoning and perspectives to prepare you to prevent a crash in real life.

Yet another explanation is that stories convey lessons and information.[9] Why learn the hard way through personal experience? If you want to know how to spear a buffalo, ask grandpa to tell the story—of the hapless warrior trampled doing it the wrong way and the hero that fed the tribe doing it the right way. Stories offer an efficient way to package hard-won experience. They simplify and streamline. They serve as easy-to-recall models or mnemonics.[10] And in that way, they deliver information more efficiently than just a lot of facts.

Still another explanation is that they offer entertainment. Tens of thousands of years ago, a mastery of any art, funny or sublime, could have been taken by a prospective mate as a sign of mental fitness. (Who doesn't love the storyteller at the party?) Perhaps, writes philosopher scientist Denis Dutton, "The mind is best seen as a gaudy, over-powered home entertainment system, evolved to help our stone-age ancestors to attract, amuse, and bed each other."[11]

NATURALLY SELECTED

Scientists keep wondering, though: Where's the data to prove such explanations? Nobody has a final answer. But many of the answers are intriguing. As an example, consider the work of anthropologists, specifically a group of experts studying storytelling among the few hunter-gatherer groups still on the planet. Their findings suggest that stories were critical to the survival of social groups—and in some cases still are.

Daniel Smith at University College London and others have studied the Agta people in the Philippines. The Agta live on rivers and along the coast in a remote, roadless forest in northeast Luzon. Their hunter-gatherer forte is fishing. They also hunt game, collect honey, harvest wild plants, and trade with locals for rice. Like other hunter-gatherer groups worldwide, they don't tell the same kinds of stories as those common among more recent farming cultures. Smith's team found that the Agta tell parables weighted heavily with messages about foraging, sex equality, and egalitarianism.

Smith's team found, in fact, that 70 percent of the Agta's stories feature cooperative social behavior. One story has it that the sun (male) and moon (female) had a fight over who would light up the sky. The pair proved equally strong. So, in the end, they stopped fighting. They split the duty, one taking the day, the other the night. What does this convey to youngsters in Agta culture? Boys and girls are equal, and they thrive when they cooperate. Other Agta stories have similar themes. In other words, Smith's team found that, as in other hunter-gatherer communities, the Agta stories promote group sharing more than fighting.

That aligns with the work of researchers on other hunter-gatherer groups. But the Smith team then wanted to know how the faculty of storytelling evolved to be so strong. To answer that question, they first wanted to gauge the popularity of storytelling and storytellers among the Agta. They found that the Agta favored storytelling as a skill twice as much as the next-most-valued skill, bringing home the most fish. They also asked 291 Agta people to name five campmates they would like to live with. The Agta nominated skilled storytellers (more often women) nearly twice as often as less skilled ones.

This is remarkable. Consuming stories was valued more than consuming food. Smith and his team then went even further. They studied the levels of group cooperation in each Agta camp to see if there was a link. Their finding: The higher the proportion of skilled storytellers in a camp, the greater the camp's level of cooperation. Smith's team even ran a game to quantify cooperation levels. They offered 290 Agta adults the chance to decide, when given 10 successive helpings of rice, whether to keep or share each one. The impulse to share, it was assumed, would be a gauge of the strength of a culture of cooperation.

The result? The higher the camp's score on cooperation, the more people in each camp shared the rice, a treasured commodity. As individuals, people being people, some players didn't share at all. But overall, the Agta shared 37 percent of their helpings. The level of storytelling and the level of sharing were correlated. Smith's team thus inferred that the facility for storytelling and social cooperation evolved together, one reinforcing the other.

To close the loop on their work, the researchers wanted to know if people with the top storytelling skills were favored reproductively. Did they have more kids? So the team looked at the number of children in each camp's family. The skilled storytellers, on average, had 0.53 more children than other Agta.[12] You can in turn infer that natural selection (a higher birth rate among storytellers) was a mechanism to assure that over the most recent 100,000 years of human evolution—5,000 generations—the story facility grew ever stronger.

Of course, times have changed. People farm now. They live in cities. They don't tell so many cooperation stories. Nobody needs to favor mating with storytellers to promote group (and in turn their own) survival. So does the Agta research continue to explain the draw of stories today?

John Donahue and Melanie Green at the University of North Carolina and State University of New York at Buffalo did a study in 2016 that suggests the answer could be yes. They found that, in an experiment with 155 students, the women found men who were good at storytelling to be more attractive as long-term mates. The hunter-gatherer impulse, the data hint, may still persist. The results for men were neutral. Still, Donahue and Green suggested from further analysis that storytelling ability increases people's perceived status.[13]

That finding certainly aligns with the cocktail-party observation that, all else being equal, storytellers ride high in the social herd. In any case, the ability to tell and comprehend stories—and to desire and like them—is alive and well today, no matter the evolutionary reason.[14]

GROWTH REWARDS

The mosaic of brain circuits that lights up during stories comprises a set of regions that scientists call the "default mode network." All humans rely on this network for both producing and comprehending stories. Technically, the key story-processing regions are the temporoparietal junction (TPJ), angular gyrus, temporal poles, posterior medial cortex (PMC), and medial prefrontal cortex (mPFC).[15] You'll recognize the TPJ as the premiere region for mind-reading from the last chapter.

"Default," to clear up any confusion, is a misnomer. The network got its name when earlier scientists scanned the brains of people "at rest." The people in fMRI machines lay in the dark. They were not given any task—no reading or word problems or videos. The scientists presumed that the images revealed the firing in people's brains at a baseline, with nothing going on.

We now know, however, that the "resting" brain stays busy all the time. It fires like crazy with daydreaming, mind wandering, mind-reading, and more. Researchers can see the busyness. The default region "at rest" devours oxygen and so bristles with activity in fMRI scans. Scientists have learned that the resting brain does not default to anything like a computer that's gone to sleep. Still, their "default" name stuck.[16]

The default network lights up both for stories as short as those from Ventura and as long as Alcott's. Research shows something else happening. As the narrative engages the default network, it engages multiple regions in the reward circuit.[17] The two don't work independently. They appear to act in concert, as connected networks across the brain talking to each other, spiking desire and spurring pleasure.[18]

That raises a question related to a point I made in chapter 4 about negative emotion: Just how can unpleasant stories be rewarding? Why would the brain reward readers with pleasure for sticking with them? How, for instance, does Alcott get you to stick with her story, which you can tell will turn out sad? Think about this as you read further:

> He seemed to cling to life, as if it were rich in duties and delights, and he had learned the secret of content[ment]. The only time I saw his composure disturbed, was when my surgeon brought another to examine John, who scrutinized their faces with an anxious look, asking of the elder: "Do you think I shall pull through, sir?"
>
> [The doctor:] "I hope so, my man."

The simple answer for why we feel the urge to keep reading might be that Alcott's setup begs the universal story question: "What comes next?" You're curious. But the more likely one is that both good and bad stories promise answers that will provide learning. In that way, both comedy and tragedy reward. Ironically, as you know from your own reading, tragedies written well may reward much more than stories that are just entertaining.

To understand this better, Ulrike Altmann and others at the Free University of Berlin looked specifically into readers' reactions to negative stories. They asked 24 people to passively read 80 unpleasant stories while in the fMRI. An example of a decidedly ugly one: "A farmer steered his harvester into a cornfield where his children were playing hide-and-seek. Suddenly the machine seemed stuck, so he got off to find the fault. When he realized that he had run over his children, he took his own life."

That's a distressing story. How could it be rewarding? Here's the surprising yet illuminating finding: When people said they liked unpleasant stories, their fMRI brain scans showed firing in the regions for mind-reading (the TPJ again). Apparently, these 24 people were inferring what the farmer was thinking and in turn making deep social connections to him. Altmann and her team concluded that both positive and negative stories spur empathy and moral reasoning, and that makes them appealing in their potential for spurring growth, if in a tragic way.[19]

MOTIVATING CUES

Here's another question about rewards in stories. In workaday writing, you're rarely going to tell long and involved stories. You'll tell short ones, fragments, or you'll relate pithy, illustrative scenes like entrepreneur Ventura's snapshot of his 23-year-old life. How does that affect rewards? As it turns out, research shows that anecdotes, jokes, case studies, scenes, full stories, single episodes—all of them signal potential rewards to readers.

Even a single story component will fire up story circuitry in the brain.[20] Though not wholly developed, fragments can still prompt the reward circuit to ready itself for the potential for a full story. The signal is an incentive for readers to keep reading, a cue like the tick of the metronome that made Pavlov's dogs salivate. Whether or not there's a grandiose payoff is another question. You salivate at the story cue.

To illustrate how brief you can make a story, even one with a beginning, middle, and end, here's John McPhee, in *Basin and Range,* tired from a day of geologic fieldwork in Nevada: "In the dark, we drove back the way we had come, over the painted cattle guards and past jackrabbits dancing in the road, pitch-dark, and suddenly a Black Angus was there, standing broadside, middle of the road. With a scream of brakes, we stopped. The animal stood still, thinking, its eyes unmoving—a wall of beef. We moved slowly after that."[21]

In just four sentences, McPhee treats us to the four critical parts of a story: the setup, the development, the climax, and the denouement. The mere sign of a plotline—in this case, a remote drive in the dark—gets your default network going.[22] In partnership with the dopamine-driven reward circuit, it gets readers to weigh the story's promise. The circuit's assessment produces the motivating chemical release to coax you to stick with the story—even before you know about that wall of beef.

A longer story still has the potential to have more motivating power. Here's Alcott again, in her story's next phase:

The next night, as I went my rounds with Dr. P., I happened to ask [him] which man in the room probably suffered most; and, to my great surprise, he glanced at John: "Every breath he draws is like a stab; for the ball pierced the left lung, broke a rib, and did no end of damage here and there . . . he must lie on his wounded back or suffocate. It will be a hard struggle."

Nurse Alcott: "You don't mean he must die, Doctor?"

"Bless you there's not the slightest hope for him; and you'd better tell him so before long; women have a way of doing such things comfortably, so I leave it to you. He won't last more than a day or two, at furthest."

POWER COUPLING

What's happening, and where, in your default mode network when you read a story like that? What accounts for the power of the story? The biggest factor appears to be the extensive and reliable coupling of Alcott's default mode network with yours. As a writer, she couldn't have found another strategy to produce such an extensive neural pattern to drive engagement.[23] That's why using stories gives you a strategy to elevate your writing from merely informative to wildly engaging.

Several teams of scientists have done a series of experiments to investigate the strength of the coupling pattern. One stream of research shows that the pattern is almost contagious. It surfaces not just between writer and reader. It surfaces in the minds of people even when they listen to a story by someone who heard the story from someone else.[24] What's more, the pattern doesn't vary across peoples or languages. When you tell your kids a tale from Dr. Seuss in English, they exhibit a brain pattern that's just the same as when Chinese parents tell the tale to their children in Chinese.

A team led by Jonas Kaplan at the University of Southern California looked into this universal effect. They condensed 40 blog stories into 145- to 155-word paragraphs. Each story was a personal drama highlighting behavior some might find objectionable—cheating on a spouse, crossing a picket line, getting into a fistfight. They then translated the stories into three sets, one English, one Chinese, one Farsi. Finally, they asked three groups of 26 native speakers, one each from the United States, China, and Iran, to read them while in the fMRI scanner.

The result was consistent: No matter the readers' language, no matter their native country, the pattern of their brain firing was the same. The coupling, the mirroring, persisted. That's not to say the scans were identical. Nor was the intensity of firing in the default network everywhere equal. Still, the same brain tissue that processes meaning swung into action for every reader.[25]

So much so that researchers elsewhere have succeeded in predicting from fMRI images which story people are reading. Leila Wehbe and others at Carnegie Mellon and other universities used machine learning to train a model to make those predictions. They first gathered data by having people read a chapter from *Harry Potter and the Sorcerer's Stone*. The model captured 195 "features" of the text, from actions to the presence of characters. After training, the model could predict, with 74 percent accuracy, which of two passages people were reading. On top of that, the team could say which brain regions encoded specific information, such as the identity of each character.[26]

STRATEGY ON STRATEGY

Beyond the robustness of this coupling, and along with the engagement of the reward circuit at the same time, other factors account for the power of story to grab readers. At the top of the list, as you're experiencing with Alcott's story, is the force of emotion. Mikkel Wallentin and his colleagues at Aarhus University in Denmark demonstrated this when they had people read "The Ugly Duckling." The classic Danish story by Hans Christian Andersen, 3,100 words long, abounds with tension, notably the anguish you feel as the oddball duckling endures rounds of abuse.

A familiar early passage: "The ducks nipped him, and the hens pecked him, and the girl who fed them kicked him with her foot."

Of course, the ending is happy, and has emotional force, too: "It was no longer the reflection of a clumsy, dirty, gray bird, ugly and offensive. He himself was a swan!"

Twenty-six people listened to those lines while in an fMRI scanner. Sure enough—even though everyone knew the story—they responded to the ebb and flow of the emotions. In the passages about both the duckling's hurtful experience and the swan's vindication, the amygdala lit up.[27]

Wallentin and his colleagues highlight how winning over readers with a keep-it-story-driven strategy leads you naturally into winning with multiple strategies at the same time, in this case keeping-it-stirring. The same goes for research by a team led by Diana Tamir at Princeton University. Tamir's team showed how much the social factor counts, in particular the presence of a person in the story.

In her group's research, Tamir asked people to read three kinds of excerpts from fiction and nonfiction: passages with vivid scenes featuring other people, passages without those vivid scenes or people, or passages describing what people were thinking. The brain's social network lit up only for the passages with people. The team's research specifically showed that readers were simulating the actions of people in the text and inferring those people's thoughts.[28]

Take stock of the impact of more than one strategy playing as you continue with Alcott:

> I could have sat down on the spot and cried heartily, if I had not learned the wisdom of bottling up one's tears for leisure moments.... I could not give him up so soon.... It was an easy thing for Dr. P. to say: "Tell him he must die," but a cruelly hard thing to do, and by no means as "comfortable" as he politely suggested.
>
> I had not the heart to do it then, and privately indulged the hope that some change for the better might take place, in spite of gloomy prophesies; so, rendering my task unnecessary.

You get a feeling for how your circuitry is firing, in ebbs and flows, just like Alcott's must have during the writing.

You may not have such gripping material, but you can still put multiple strategies into play in your own writing. When you do with a longer story, you reap more rewards for your reader. The intensity of those rewards starts to become apparent in research by Jonas Kaplan's team. They examined how the firing of the default network varies as a story proceeds. They found that, as people read further and further into a story, the default mode network fired more intensely. This was true even though they asked people to read stories that were only 150 words long.

The more a story unfolds, the more you get wrapped up in it. Here's Alcott as if to prove it:

> The Doctor's words caused me to reproach myself with neglect, not of any real duty perhaps, but of those little cares and kindnesses that solace homesick spirits, and make the heavy hours pass easier.
>
> John looked lonely and forsaken just then, as he sat with bent head, hands folded on his knee, and no outward sign of suffering, till, looking nearer, I saw great tears roll down and drop upon the floor. It was a new sight there; for, though I had seen many suffer, some swore, some groaned, most endured silently, but none wept. Yet it did not seem weak, only very touching, and straightway my fear vanished.... I said, "Let me help you bear it, John."

Erez Simony at Princeton (on the Hasson team) looked further into the force a story accumulates as it gets longer. The Simony team asked 36 people to listen to a seven-minute story from the "The Moth" storytelling event in New York. The story, "Pie Man," by Jim O'Grady, opens with an unidentified student mashing a cream pie into the face of a college dean. This happens just as O'Grady, a student newspaper journalist, asks the dean about a controversial admission policy. (From there, the plot thickens. Find it on YouTube.[29])

The Simony team showed that, over seven minutes, the strength of interaction among nodes of the default mode network went up and up. That extended the Kaplan team's finding. They also showed how much story structure serves as a trigger. They found the high-level story structure and meaning—sequential narrative structure, not solo sentences, paragraphs, or scenes—drove the accumulating intensity.[30] So again, a McPhee-like wall-of-beef anecdote works well to clinch reader engagement. But a longer pie-in-the-face story does more. Readers become more and more engaged while integrating earlier facts and events with later ones.

MEDIA MATTERS, NOT

In today's world, you might wonder how a writer of stories can compete with video stories. Is it possible? Offhand, you might not think so, and that's what I thought. But scientists exploring that question have found the opposite. It doesn't matter how your audience processes a story—while reading, listening, watching a video, or watching someone draw or pantomime.[31] The default network erupts while interpreting meaning in the same way.

That's not to say neurons for hearing don't swing into action when people listen to the sound. Or sight neurons don't flare during watching. But across a high-level subset of the default mode network, *the meaning* drives the action. The sound and images offer great accompaniment, but they work though circuits other than those producing meaning.[32] So if you've been worried about video enjoying a monopoly on communication in the future, you can worry a bit less.

Daniel Richardson and a team from University College London looked specifically into the question of whether video is superior in transmitting meaning. They compared reactions to text (audio) and video stories by 95 people. The stories came from eight pieces of great fiction, varying from *Great Expectations* and *The Da Vinci Code* to *The Silence of the Lambs* and *A Song of Ice and Fire (Game of Thrones)*.

On the one hand, they asked people to *say* how much a story engaged them. On the other, they *measured* how much a story moved them, according to physiological signs of arousal. The results were split but intriguing. Data showed that people paid better attention to the videos and showed more understanding. They also reported 15 percent more engagement.

But here was the surprise: Sensors on their wrists gave a different picture. Their average heart rate was about two beats higher per minute while listening, their skin conductance (from perspiration) was greater, and they were about a third of a degree warmer. The data, in spite of what the people thought, showed they were aroused *physiologically more* with the text.[33]

Besides showing that text remains alive and well in competing with video, the results are a reminder that unconscious emotions and conscious feelings are separate in the brain. Unconscious emotions don't necessarily surface as "felt."[34] And so, without your knowing it, you may behave in line with just your unconscious. Your reward circuit may even swing into action without your feeling conscious pleasure.

As Alcott moves to the climax of her story about John, you certainly don't need a video to feel emotion:

> He seemed to read the thought that troubled me, as he spoke so hopefully when there was no hope, for he suddenly added:

"This is my first battle; do they think it's going to be my last?"

"I'm afraid they do, John."

It was the hardest question I had ever been called upon to answer; doubly hard with those clear eyes fixed on mine, forcing a truthful answer by their own truth.

STORIES FOR GOOD

Alcott makes the case for the power of story: If you work with protagonists faced with troubles, if you chronicle how they endure trials, if you develop plotlines that prompt their realizations and reveal resolutions you take possession of the reader's brain. You hook, engage, and please. That's why so many books are written on story craft, even if it's only one of many strategies to engage readers.

Besides engagement, however, stories have other benefits. One of them is to help readers remember your message better. Mar, at York University, reviewed 37 studies with 33,000 participants.[35] The data were consistent: "What we found is that there was a clear and distinctive advantage across all the studies for information that's presented as a narrative, both with respect to comprehension and memory," he says. "There is a great deal of quantitative evidence that there are advantages to employing a story format judiciously." Readers, in other words, remember more facts woven into a narrative than into an essay.

Other scientists have shown that stories are more effective in changing behavior than are explanatory texts.[36] Sheila

Murphy and others at the University of Southern California investigated how to increase women's compliance in getting regular Pap smears to avoid cervical cancer. To do so, they tested two 11-minute health-education films. One featured local doctors speaking about evidence for the benefits of Pap smears using charts and figures. The other featured a story, "The Tamale Lesson," about a group of mothers and daughters celebrating a birthday in the fictional Romero family.

Both films gave the same facts about how the human papillomavirus causes most cervical cancers. They also both explained why women need Pap tests even if they aren't sexually active, and even if they're as young as nine years old. You can by now guess the result: The story group, tested after watching the film, learned significantly more than the other "just the facts," group. They also reported a greater inclination to get cervical cancer screening.[37]

Work by Kurt Braddock and James Dillard of Pennsylvania State University further explains this result. They analyzed 74 previous studies and found that narratives caused change in four variables: beliefs, attitudes, intentions, and behaviors. People tended to align—or realign—their views not so much with the facts but with the people portrayed in the narrative. Once again, people more often get engaged with people, not facts. The research showed that the change didn't depend on which type of media the stories came through, text, video, or audio.[38]

Among the professionals who take advantage of the suasion of stories are lawyers. In jury trials, lawyers have learned—and research confirms—that jurors more often reason through to verdicts with narrative. To confirm this, a team led by Jaime

Castrellon at Duke University examined fMRI scans of mock jury members' brains. The resulting neural patterns showed that story reasoning better explained people's thought processes than an accumulation of the facts, or the weight of the evidence. Stories, in other words, guided reasoning about the probability that a defendant committed a crime.[39]

Professionals who could take more advantage of story suasion include businesspeople. Researchers who looked at two kinds of business crowdfunding campaigns found that campaigns with richer narratives earned higher marks in terms of entrepreneur credibility, legitimacy, and intentions of people to invest and share.[40] Stories, in other words, influence funding success.[41] Investors follow the story, factual or not, to justify their decisions.[42]

Readers are so inclined to give in to the influence of stories that they may lapse in their judgment of the credibility of the story. Melanie Green and Timothy Brock, then at The Ohio State University, conducted research that highlighted this effect. They asked 69 students to read a story about the murder of a child, Katie, who was shopping at a local mall with her college-age sister. It was a gripping (and true) tale. They then quizzed people afterward to ask how transported they felt. To test if the degree of transportation affected people's powers of discrimination, they also gave them a script of the story and asked them to circle any "false notes" they could find.

"False notes" were facts or beliefs Green and Brock had planted that didn't ring true with the overall story—details that contradicted each other or didn't make sense. The false notes task was aimed at seeing whether readers let the plot and character so influence them that they would ignore contradictory facts. The results confirmed their hunch. The people who were highly transported noted far fewer false notes than the less transported people.[43] That seems to confirm the potential for abuse captured in the old adage about storytelling: Don't let the facts get in the way of a good story.

Green and Brock showed one more thing about story persuasiveness: Stories change the way readers feel and reason, at least temporarily, *after* they read the story. When they asked people if attacks in public places are likely, the more transported readers were more likely to agree.

Other researchers have shown the influencing effect of stories comes out afterward in other ways. Maj-Britt Isberner and others at the University of Kassel in Germany showed that when readers feel transported in a story with a strong protagonist, they feel stronger. Isberner's team asked 77 Germans (55 women, 21 men, 1 unreported) to listen to or watch two kinds of narratives. One kind included high "self-efficacy" protagonists—Pocahontas, Merida from *Brave*, and Belle from *Beauty and the Beast*. The other included the reverse—Cinderella, Rapunzel, and Snow White.

The people either listened to 1,000-word excerpts or watched Disney film clips. As you probably know, the first set of stories features protagonists who stand up for themselves, and the second, those who act passively and submissively. And as you might guess, the highly transported participants, after viewing or reading the high self-efficacy stories, reported a significantly higher sense of self-efficacy compared to a week before the study. Those who reported low transportation did not.[44] Not all readers reacted the same way, of course, but stories influenced them all.[45] You can see that the engagement you gain from readers of stories persists well after they finish them.

Depending on your line of work, you may not have ready story material for your writing. You might in turn wonder if using fictional "what if" stories (per chapter 5) might work but give you a second-rate effect. But that's not apparently a worry. Franziska Hartung and others at Radboud University in the Netherlands alternately told 1,800 readers, in advance, that the stories they were about to read were either true or not. The reaction by readers was the same: People felt equally immersed. And this was for stories that were *identical*. What mattered was not readers' knowledge of truthfulness but the narrative style.[46]

Alcott may have known the same thing through experience. Her narrative style, not just her other talents, allowed her to break out as a writer. In her story, she doesn't argue about the woe of war. She doesn't reason with any reader. She won over the American public during the United States' most deadly war ever with a story. And she had more to say:

I had been summoned to many death beds in my life, but to none that made my heart ache as it did then . . . even while he spoke, over his face I saw the gray veil falling that no human hand can lift. I sat down by him, wiped the drops from his forehead, stirred the air about him with the slow wave of a fan, and waited to help him die. . . .

I thought him nearly gone, and had just laid down the fan, believing its help to be no longer needed, when suddenly he rose up in his bed, and cried out with a bitter cry that broke the silence, sharply startling every one with its agonized appeal:

"For God's sake, give me air!"

STORY DRIVE

So, we now know that, in the classic sense, the phases of story include setup, buildup, climax, and aftermath. At this point, Alcott was at the climax. But you can use any of the phases, or all of them, even in basic essays and reports, to transform otherwise clear and informative writing into engaging and rewarding prose. Here are five top tactics, harnessing what we know from science:

Protagonists rule: Feature a person readers can care about. If you're writing about yourself, show how you faced a trying time (Alcott). If you're writing about biology, feature a striving scientist (the researchers in this book). If you don't have a real character to feature, invent one (Jane).

Robin Boneck, David Christensen, and Gerald Calvasina start an article in *CPA Journal:* "In 2014, Paul Somers was fired from Digital Realty for reporting to senior management that his supervisor eliminated some internal controls, in violation of the Sarbanes-Oxley Act (SOX). Instead of filing a complaint with the SEC [Securities and Exchange Commission] within 180 days of the alleged retaliation, Somers waited seven months before suing his employer."[47]

"There's no mystery about what makes stories so fascinating," notes York University's Mar. "They're about people, and people are what we care about."[48]

Susan Cain, author of *Quiet,* starts: "The date: 1902. The place: Harmony Church, Missouri, a tiny, dot-on-the-map town on a floodplain a hundred miles from Kansas City. Our young protagonist: a good-natured but insecure high school student named Dale."[49]

Reveal struggle: Highlight Jane's (or Ventura's or Louisa May's) challenges. Focus on life- or perspective-changing junctures. These plot points pivot readers toward your message.

"Jason Murdoch was an inpatient at a rehabilitation center in San Diego. After a serious head injury in a car accident near the Mexican border, he had been in a semiconscious state of vigilant coma (also called akinetic mutism) for nearly three months . . ." So starts V. S. Ramachandran in a chapter in *The Tell-Tale Brain.*[50]

"Napoleon Bonaparte said in 1805: 'All empires die of indigestion.' In trying to amass ever more territory, they consume more than they can handle. Napoleon got indigestion himself in Russia."[51] So writes Richard D'Aveni in *Strategic Capitalism.*

D'Aveni and Ramachandran both capture your attention by putting people's future on the line in the face of a struggle. Ramachandran then segues into people's capacity for introspection. D'Aveni segues into the decline of the U.S. from geopolitical overreach.

Build an arc. Show the people you write about advancing and growing. Readers want to see people taking charge of their lives. In a classic story arc, the protagonist(s) tries first one, then a second, and even a third way to overcome a challenge—until a fresh realization comes to her (at the climax) that leads to a resolution, good or bad.

In his classic speech on citizenship, Teddy Roosevelt wrote an arc in one sentence: "The credit belongs to the man who is actually in the arena, whose face is marred by dust and sweat and blood; who strives valiantly; who . . . knows great enthusiasms, the great devotions; who spends himself in a worthy cause; who at the best knows in the end the triumph of high achievement, and who at the worst, if he fails, at least fails while daring greatly, so that his place shall never be with those cold and timid souls who neither know victory nor defeat."[52] That passage, from 1910, still resonates, and now you know why.

Upton Sinclair crafted an arc in a "what-if" scenario in *The Brass Check,* his polemic against yellow journalism in the 1920s: "Imagine yourself a poor devil, caught in a set of circumstances which cause the city editor of some newspaper, after five minutes consideration, to make up his mind that you are guilty of a crime! Trial by a city editor in five minutes, and execution in columns of illustrated slander—that is our American system of jurisprudence."[53]

Alcott hit the peak of her arc after John's death:

He never spoke again, but to the end held my hand close, so close that when he was asleep at last, I could not draw it away. [The orderly] helped me, warning me as he did so that it was unsafe for dead and living flesh to lie so long together; but though my hand was strangely cold and stiff, and four white marks remained across its back, even when warmth and color had returned elsewhere, I could not but be glad that, through its touch, the presence of human sympathy, perhaps, had lightened that hard hour."

Spotlight realization. Clinch passages with insights, just as Roosevelt, Sinclair, and Alcott do. Highlight for readers your *intended* message point. Don't let them choose on their own any one of a list of messages each plot point could convey.

An easy composition mistake: Letting the most gripping angle of a story take the reader (and often you as the writer) off your intended point. Step in as the narrator to foreground the angle you want your story to take. Fiction writers may leave the message of a story up to readers. But nonfiction writers articulate the message to make the story's purpose plain.

Alcott writes:

> I felt a tender sort of pride in my lost patient; for he looked a most heroic figure, lying there stately and still as the statue of some young knight asleep upon his tomb. The lovely expression which so often beautifies dead faces, soon replaced the marks of pain, and I longed for those who loved him best to see him when half an hour's acquaintance with Death had made them friends.

Wrap up with meaning. Bring closure, a parting shot, meaning piled on meaning, a larger realization built on small ones. This might come in the conclusion.

In his account of life as a seaman, Joseph Conrad recounts a rescue of sailors from a wreck. After a harrowing tale of specifics, in which he spotlights many realizations, he wraps up by scorning the sea as an object of romance: "My conception of its magnanimous greatness was gone. And I looked upon the true sea—the sea that plays with men till their hearts are broken, and wears stout ships to death. Nothing can touch the brooding bitterness of its heart."[54]

Ramachandran did the same in his story about the coma patient—remarkably, Jason Murdoch, albeit normally unresponsive, could talk to his father on the phone, so long as his father was not in the room. Ramachandran marvels: "The self is not a monolithic entity it believes itself to be.... What the neurology tells us is that the self consists of many components, and the notion of one unitary self may well be an illusion."[55]

Alcott finishes at the moment an eagerly expected letter arrives from John's mother, just an hour too late for him to read it:

> I kissed this good son for her sake, and laid the letter in his hand ... he would not be without some token of the lover which makes life beautiful and outlives death. Then I left him, glad to have known so genuine a man, and carrying with me an enduring memory of the brave Virginia blacksmith, as he lay serenely waiting for the dawn of that long day which knows no night.[56]

People are pushovers when it comes to stories. They can't help it because stories offer so many rewards. Rewards from simplicity. From specifics. From surprise. From emotion. From all the writing strategies. They allow us to become engaged, if not transported, with the unfolding of plot, the stream of cause and effect, the intensity of mind-reading. The story offers a premier way to flourish in your writing, to break out with influence and even thought leadership.

There's an old writer's aphorism that applies to story but also to all of writing: "Write to please yourself." Now you know why that resonates. When you write to please yourself, you are writing to the same brain that pleases readers. This is not a selfish act. It is a selfless one. Readers don't stick with you because they like your "writing style." They stick with you because they love the way you reward yourself—and them— as humans.

REWARDS FROM WITHIN

What do the eight strategies add up to? They offer a science-based approach to writing to engage readers, of course. The research behind them shows why the time-tested strategies of great writers work. But they also offer a science-based approach to understanding people. They outline a way to grasp and tap the motivation for all human striving—yours and that of the people you're writing for.

Scientists have laid the groundwork to reveal a set of universal, hardwired impulses that drive that motivation. To compose like a pro, you have to tap the human desire for the simple and specific, surprising and stirring, seductive and smart, social and story-driven. When you do, you play to impulses that stimulate wanting. That induce liking. That drive learning. You motivate readers to read on and on.

You then have the potential of producing great writing, to break through with influence for your point of view. That will allow you to win over audiences that matter to you. Of course, you may not win any prizes. Those are reserved for notable journalists and columnists and narrative nonfiction authors. They are especially reserved for fiction authors, who still hold the high ground in composing to engage and move readers.

But if you practice the eight strategies, you can aspire to produce writing that stands out in your field. That includes everyday emails and reports and blogs. It includes longer works, op-ed articles, and online articles for the public. It even includes monographs and books for general readers. You will succeed with your writing by transforming it with the same tactics as the experts. You will flourish as a professional as you communicate with impact with the help of science.

Science has its limits, though. True enough, researchers have access to high-tech tools, polished procedures, and clever theories to explain the workings of the mind. They give us pictures and data to describe mental faculties we could only have imagined before. They give us research to support this unique menu of strategies to make better writing decisions. But they don't have any more direct, personal access to humanness—to the wants and needs of the human mind—than you do.

You, like everyone else, have inherited a legacy of the universal mind. You come equipped with a low-tech but high-powered tool: intuition. You have within your head the ability to tap that evolutionarily derived intuition directly. You can always ask, What's the primal mind yearning for? Answering that question—that's the soulful part of writing.

When you sit down to write, in other words, you enter the realm of art and science as one. Ironically, over the centuries, artists have looked down on the relevance of scientists, and scientists have looked down on the relevance of artists. Now that you've read this book, you must think: How crazy! Both realms, united, let you judge the best way to trade off—and harmonize—one writing strategy with another.

Artists and scientists are in league with each other in this task. Some of the most revered artists of the past have even made their life's mission to merge science into their art. Think Leonardo da Vinci, engineer and anatomist, painter and sculptor. Scientists and artists ache for the same prize as that genius of the Renaissance: to fathom the human condition and serve others with the fruits of their insights.

We're all in this together. If you're a student of brain science, you're a student of human nature. If you're a student of writing, you're a student of human nature. If you're a student of art, you're a student of human nature. The intellect and the imagination, the head and the heart—all work within us to the same end.

So let science and art both help you make writing decisions, confident you're listening to the full wisdom of a brain polished over a thousand generations before you. Just which word or metaphor or emotion works best in the next sentence? Let both science and art guide you in answering that question. Let them both help you reap the rewards of following the ancient—and relentlessly rewarding—echoes of your muse.

> *... light the fire;*
> *every syllable spelled out is a spark.*
> —VICTOR HUGO[1]

ACKNOWLEDGMENTS

However open-minded you are when you're writing a book, you're stuck for days and weeks in the same chair with the same point of view. You look out the same window. You study research in the same subject. You consult the same cadre of scholars. From this self-created intellectual cave, you come up with some great thoughts. But at least with your early drafts you also come up with some dumb ideas. You can't help it.

You need friends and colleagues to shine light where you see only dark. So I'm in debt to a lot of people for providing that light—and doing a lot more—to make this book worthwhile. If you read the preface, you know that John Butman was an early, crucial advisor. John got me to step much further afield than I was planning. John got me to think outside the cave.

Once I was seeing daylight, Sarah Moughty and the editors at *Harvard Business Review* embraced my work. They asked me to draft an article for the magazine. Sarah and others made sure I highlighted the most useful insights for everyday professionals. I'm indebted to them. They got me launched.

Hundreds of psychologists, cognitive scientists, and neuroscientists, that cadre of experts in the global research academy, deserve the bulk of the credit for the most intriguing insights.

I relied on over 500 of their journal articles to piece together the science behind the reward circuit and the eight writing strategies. Many of their articles are cited in the endnotes.

Eight scientists shared their thoughts in interviews. Among them, I first want to thank Kent Berridge at the University of Michigan, whose breakout work on the reward circuit opened my eyes to the book's core insight. Seven others helped me go much further: Mark Beeman at Northwestern University; Ben Bergen at the University of California, San Diego; Francesca Citron at Lancaster University (UK); David Dodell-Feder at the University of Rochester; Art Glenberg at Arizona State University; Raymond Mar at York University (Canada); and Piotr Winkielman at the University of California, San Diego.

Four friends and writing colleagues read an early version of the manuscript. They gave me a big lift when I really needed it. They not only put up with many half-formed thoughts, they pointed out where I was losing readers, and they even let me steal some great turns of phrase. I can't thank them enough: Emily Archer, Herb Archer, David Locke, and Jon Vara. Thanks for all those pencil marks, guys!

All great books rely on the skills—and goodwill—of an entire publishing team. Thank goodness for them! At the head of the line comes Alice Martell, my incomparable agent. Alice got me to produce a knockout book proposal, she sang the praises of the book, and she found a terrific home for the book at HarperCollins Leadership. Thanks, Alice!

At HarperCollins, Tim Burgard, my editor, saw the value of a science-based writing book right away. He boosted my confidence in its value and guided me in making the book even better. Special thanks to Aryn Van Dyke for running the marketing at HarperCollins and to Beth Kessler, Mikayla Butchart, and Kim Nir on the production team at Neuwirth & Associates. So to all of you, thanks so much.

Finally, my wife, Suzanne, plays the role of writer's spouse with inborn talent as critic, therapist, and cheerleader. She knows when to offer kind words (often), indulge me with her patience when I think out loud (too often), and correct me when my point of view is clouded by too much time in the cave (more often than I'd like to admit). Couldn't live without her. Love you, Sue. You are the reward of my life.

ESSENTIAL REFERENCES

Introduction: Reward Your Reader

Berridge, Kent C. "Evolving Concepts of Emotion and Motivation." *Frontiers in Psychology* 9 (September 2018): 1647.

Berridge, Kent C., and Morten L. Kringelbach. "Building a Neuroscience of Pleasure and Well-Being." *Psychology of Well-Being: Theory, Research and Practice* 1 (2011): 1–26.

————. "Pleasure Systems in the Brain." *Neuron* 86, no. 3 (2015): 646–64.

Gazzaniga, Michael, Richard Ivry, and George Mangun. *Cognitive Neuroscience: The Biology of the Mind* (New York: W. W. Norton, 2019).

Jung-Beeman, Mark. "Bilateral Brain Processes for Comprehending Natural Language." *Trends in Cognitive Sciences* 9, no. 11 (2005): 512–18.

Kringelbach, Morten L., and Kent C. Berridge. "The Affective Core of Emotion: Linking Pleasure, Subjective Well-Being, and Optimal Metastability in the Brain." *Emotion Review* 9, no. 3 (2017): 191–99.

————. "The Joyful Mind." *Scientific American* 307, no. 2 (2012): 40–45.

————. "Neuroscience of Reward, Motivation and Drive." *Advances in Motivation and Achievement: Recent Developments in Neuroscience Research on Human Motivation,* eds. S. I. Kim, J. Reeve, and M. Bong (Bingley: Emerald Group Publishing, 2016): 23–35.

Kringelbach, Morten L., Peter Vuust, and John Geake. "The Pleasure of Reading," *Interdisciplinary Science Reviews* 33, no. 4 (2008): 321–35.

Nguyen, David, Erin E. Naffziger, and Kent C. Berridge. "Positive Affect: Nature and Brain Bases of Liking and Wanting." *Current Opinion in Behavioral Sciences* 39 (March 8, 2021): 72–78.

Ratey, John J. *A User's Guide to the Brain.* (New York: Vintage, 2002).

Schultz, Wolfram. "Neuronal Reward and Decision Signals: From Theories to Data." *Physiological Reviews* 95, no. 3 (2015): 853–951.

Chapter 1: Keep It Simple

Berger, Jonah, Wendy W. Moe, and David Schweidel. "What Leads to Longer Reads? Psychological Drivers of Reading Online Content." *ACR North American Advances* (2019).

Chater, Nick. "Simplicity and the Mind." *The Psychologist* (November 1997): 495–98.

Chater, Nick, and George Loewenstein. "The Under-Appreciated Drive for Sense-Making." *Journal of Economic Behavior & Organization* 126 (2016): 137–54.

Chenier, Troy, and Piotr Winkielman. "The Origins of Aesthetic Pleasure: Processing Fluency and Affect in Judgment, Body, and the Brain." In *Neuroaesthetics,* 275-89. London: Routledge, 2009.

Hwang, Byoung-Hyoun, and Hugh Hoikwang Kim. "It Pays to Write Well." *Journal of Financial Economics* 124, no. 2 (2017): 373–94.

Jung-Beeman, Mark. "Bilateral Brain Processes for Comprehending Natural Language." *Trends in Cognitive Sciences* 9, no. 11 (2005): 512–18.

Landwehr, Jan R., and Lisa Eckmann. "The Nature of Processing Fluency: Amplification Versus Hedonic Marking." *Journal of Experimental Social Psychology* 90 (May 25, 2020): 103997.

Mayer, Richard E., Sherry Fennell, Lindsay Farmer, and Julie Campbell. "A Personalization Effect in Multimedia Learning: Students Learn Better When Words Are in Conversational Style Rather Than Formal Style." *Journal of Educational Psychology* 96, no. 2 (2004): 389–95.

Oppenheimer, Daniel M. "Consequences of Erudite Vernacular Utilized Irrespective of Necessity: Problems with Using Long Words Needlessly." *Applied Cognitive Psychology: The Official Journal of the Society for Applied Research in Memory and Cognition* 20, no. 2 (2006): 139–56.

Winkielman, Piotr, Norbert Schwarz, Tetra Fazendeiro, and Rolf Reber. "The Hedonic Marking of Processing Fluency: Implications for Evaluative Judgment." *The Psychology of Evaluation: Affective Processes in Cognition and Emotion* 189 (January 30, 2003): 217.

Chapter 2: Keep It Specific

Bergen, Benjamin K. *Louder Than Words* (New York: Basic Books, 2012).

Berger, Jonah, Wendy W. Moe, and David Schweidel. "What Leads to Longer Reads? Psychological Drivers of Reading Online Content." *ACR North American Advances* (2019).

Costa, Vincent D., Peter J. Lang, Dean Sabatinelli, Francesco Versace, and Margaret M Bradley. "Emotional Imagery: Assessing Pleasure and Arousal in the Brain's Reward Circuitry." *Human Brain Mapping* 31, no. 9 (February 2010): 1446–57.

Fernandino, Leonardo, Jia-Qing Tong, Lisa L. Conant, Colin J. Humphries, and Jeffrey R. Binder. "Decoding the Information Structure Underlying the Neural Representation of Concepts." *Proceedings of the National Academy of Sciences* 119, no. 6 (2022): e2108091119.

Gallese, Vittorio, and George Lakoff. "The Brain's Concepts: The Role of the Sensory-Motor System in Conceptual Knowledge." *Cognitive Neuropsychology* 22, no. 3–4 (2005): 455–79.

Glenberg, Arthur M. "Few Believe the World Is Flat: How Embodiment Is Changing the Scientific Understanding of Cognition." *Canadian Journal of Experimental Psychology/Revue Canadienne de Psychologie Expérimentale* 69, no. 2 (2015): 165.

Kiefer, Markus, and Marcel Harpaintner. "Varieties of Abstract Concepts and Their Grounding in Perception or Action." *Open Psychology* 2, no. 1 (2020): 119–37.

Stins, John F., Fernando Marmolejo-Ramos, Femke Hulzinga, Eric Wenker, and Rouwen Cañal-Bruland. "Words That Move Us. The Effects of Sentences on Body Sway." *Advances in Cognitive Psychology* 13, no. 2 (2017): 156.

Van Dam, Wessel O., Shirley-Ann Rueschemeyer, and Harold Bekkering. "How Specifically Are Action Verbs Represented in the Neural Motor System: An fMRI Study." *Neuroimage* 53, no. 4 (2010): 1318–25.

Vergallito, Alessandra, Marco Alessandro Petilli, Luigi Cattaneo, and Marco Marelli. "Somatic and Visceral Effects of Word Valence, Arousal and Concreteness in a Continuum Lexical Space." *Scientific Reports* 9, no. 1 (2019): 1–10.

Zwaan, Rolf A., and Diane Pecher. "Revisiting Mental Simulation in Language Comprehension: Six Replication Attempts." *PloS ONE* 7, no. 12 (December 2012): e51382.

Chapter 3: Keep It Surprising

Berger, Jonah, and Katherine L. Milkman. "Emotion and Virality: What Makes Online Content Go Viral?" *Marketing Intelligence Review* 5, no. 1 (2013): 18–23.

Bonhage, Corinna E., Jutta L. Mueller, Angela D. Friederici, and Christian J. Fiebach. "Combined Eye Tracking and fMRI Reveals Neural Basis of Linguistic Predictions During Sentence Comprehension." *Cortex* 68 (April 2015): 33–47.

DeLong, Katherine A., Thomas P. Urbach, and Marta Kutas. "Probabilistic Word Pre-Activation During Language Comprehension Inferred from Electrical Brain Activity." *Nature Neuroscience* 8, no. 8 (2005): 1117–21.

Dessalles, Jean-Louis. "Have You Anything Unexpected to Say? The Human Propensity to Communicate Surprise and Its Role in the Emergence of

Language." Paper presented at the Evolution of Language—Proceedings of the Eighth International Conference, Utrecht, 2010.

Fouragnan, Elsa, Chris Retzler, and Marios G. Philiastides. "Separate Neural Representations of Prediction Error Valence and Surprise: Evidence from an fMRI Meta-Analysis." *Human Brain Mapping* 39, no. 7 (2018): 2887.

Kafkas, Alex, and Daniela Montaldi. "How Do Memory Systems Detect and Respond to Novelty?" *Neuroscience Letters* 680 (Febuary 3, 2018): 60–68.

Krebs, Ruth M., Dorothee Heipertz, Hartmut Schuetze, and Emrah Duzel. "Novelty Increases the Mesolimbic Functional Connectivity of the Substantia Nigra/Ventral Tegmental Area (SN/VTA) During Reward Anticipation: Evidence from High-Resolution fMRI." *Neuroimage* 58, no. 2 (June 2011): 647–55.

Rohde, Hannah, Richard Futrell, and Christopher G Lucas. "What's New? A Comprehension Bias in Favor of Informativity." *Cognition* 209 (2021): 104491.

Tapper, Andrew R., and Susanna Molas. "Midbrain Circuits of Novelty Processing." *Neurobiology of Learning and Memory* 176 (October 2020): 107323.

Chapter 4: Keep It Stirring

Citron, Francesca M. M. "Neural Correlates of Written Emotion Word Processing: A Review of Recent Electrophysiological and Hemodynamic Neuroimaging Studies." *Brain and Language* 122, no. 3 (2012): 211–26.

Citron, Francesca M. M., and Adele E. Goldberg. "Metaphorical Sentences Are More Emotionally Engaging Than Their Counterparts." *Journal of Cognitive Neuroscience* 26, no. 11 (2014): 2585–95.

Citron, Francesca M. M., Jeremie Güsten, Nora Michaelis, and Adele E. Goldberg. "Conventional Metaphors in Longer Passages Evoke Affective Brain Response." *NeuroImage* 139 (2016): 218–30.

Costa, Vincent D., Peter J. Lang, Dean Sabatinelli, Francesco Versace, and Margaret M. Bradley. "Emotional Imagery: Assessing Pleasure and Arousal in the Brain's Reward Circuitry." *Human Brain Mapping* 31, no. 9 (February 2010): 1446–57.

Damasio, Antonio, and Gil B. Carvalho. "The Nature of Feelings: Evolutionary and Neurobiological Origins." *Nature Reviews Neuroscience* 14, no. 2 (2013): 143–52.

Davis, Joshua D., Piotr Winkielman, and Seana Coulson. "Facial Action and Emotional Language: ERP Evidence That Blocking Facial Feedback Selectively Impairs Sentence Comprehension." *Journal of Cognitive Neuroscience* 27, no. 11 (2015): 2269–80.

Havas, David A., Arthur M. Glenberg, Karol A. Gutowski, Mark J. Lucarelli, and Richard J. Davidson. "Cosmetic Use of Botulinum Toxin-A Affects

Processing of Emotional Language." *Psychological Science* 21, no. 7 (July 2010): 895–900.

Oosterwijk, Suzanne, Lukas Snoek, Jurriaan Tekoppele, Lara H. Engelbert, and H. Steven Scholte. "Choosing to View Morbid Information Involves Reward Circuitry." *Scientific Reports* 10, no. 1 (2020): 1–13.

Ramachandran, V. S. *The Tell-Tale Brain: A Neuroscientist's Quest for What Makes Us Human* (New York: W. W. Norton, 2011).

Winkielman, Piotr, Seana Coulson, and Paula Niedenthal. "Dynamic Grounding of Emotion Concepts." *Philosophical Transactions of the Royal Society B: Biological Sciences* 373, no. 1752 (2018): 20170127.

Chapter 5: Keep It Seductive

FitzGibbon, Lily, Johnny King L. Lau, and Kou Murayama. "The Seductive Lure of Curiosity: Information as a Motivationally Salient Reward." *Current Opinion in Behavioral Sciences* 35 (October 1, 2020): 21–27.

Gruber, Matthias J., Bernard D. Gelman, and Charan Ranganath. "States of Curiosity Modulate Hippocampus-Dependent Learning Via the Dopaminergic Circuit." *Neuron* 84, no. 2 (2014): 486–96.

Iigaya, Kiyohito, Tobias U. Hauser, Zeb Kurth-Nelson, John P. O'Doherty, Peter Dayan, and Raymond J Dolan. "The Value of What's to Come: Neural Mechanisms Coupling Prediction Error and the Utility of Anticipation." *Science Advances* 6, no. 25 (2020): eaba3828.

Kang, Min Jeong, Ming Hsu, Ian M. Krajbich, George Loewenstein, Samuel M. McClure, Joseph Tao-yi Wang, and Colin F. Camerer. "The Wick in the Candle of Learning: Epistemic Curiosity Activates Reward Circuitry and Enhances Memory." *Psychological Science* 20, no. 8 (2009): 963–73.

Kobayashi, Kenji, and Ming Hsu. "Common Neural Code for Reward and Information Value." *Proceedings of the National Academy of Sciences* 116, no. 26 (June 11, 2019): 13061–66.

Lau, Johnny King L., Hiroki Ozono, Kei Kuratomi, Asuka Komiya, and Kou Murayama. "Shared Striatal Activity in Decisions to Satisfy Curiosity and Hunger at the Risk of Electric Shocks." *Nature Human Behaviour* 4, no. 5 (2020): 531–43.

Leavitt, Jonathan Daniel. "Motivations for Reading Stories: Hedonic Responses to Fictionality and Suspense." Dissertation, University of California, San Diego, 2013.

Li, Zhi-Wei, Neil R. Bramley, and Todd M. Gureckis. "Expectations about Future Learning Influence Moment-to-Moment Feelings of Suspense." *Cognition and Emotion* 35, no. 6 (2021): 1099–1120.

van Lieshout, Lieke L. F., Floris P. de Lange, and Roshan Cools. "Why So Curious? Quantifying Mechanisms of Information Seeking." *Current Opinion in Behavioral Sciences* 35 (October 3, 2020): 112–17.

Wassiliwizky, Eugen, Stefan Koelsch, Valentin Wagner, Thomas Jacobsen, and Winfried Menninghaus. "The Emotional Power of Poetry: Neural Circuitry, Psychophysiology and Compositional Principles." *Social Cognitive and Affective Neuroscience* 12, no. 8 (2017): 1229–40.

Chapter 6: Keep It Smart

Chesebrough, Christine B. "Conceptual Change Induced by Analogical Reasoning Sparks 'Aha!' Moments." Thesis, Drexel University, 2021.

Conrad, Erin C., Stacey Humphries, and Anjan Chatterjee. "Attitudes toward Cognitive Enhancement: The Role of Metaphor and Context." *AJOB Neuroscience* 10, no. 1 (2019): 35–47.

Jung-Beeman, Mark, Edward M. Bowden, Jason Haberman, Jennifer L. Frymiare, Stella Arambel-Liu, Richard Greenblatt, Paul J. Reber, and John Kounios. "Neural Activity When People Solve Verbal Problems with Insight." *PLoS Biol* 2, no. 4 (2004): e97.

Kizilirmak, Jasmin M, Björn H. Schott, Hannes Thuerich, Catherine M. Sweeney-Reed, Anni Richter, Kristian Folta-Schoofs, and Alan Richardson-Klavehn. "Learning of Novel Semantic Relationships Via Sudden Comprehension Is Associated with a Hippocampus-Independent Network." *Consciousness and Cognition* 69 (2019): 113–32.

Kounios, John, and Mark Beeman. "The Aha! Moment: The Cognitive Neuroscience of Insight." *Current Directions in Psychological Science* 18, no. 4 (2009): 210–16.

———. "The Cognitive Neuroscience of Insight." *Annual Review of Psychology* 65 (2014).

Mon, Serena K., Mira Nencheva, Francesca M. M. Citron, Casey Lew-Williams, and Adele E. Goldberg. "Conventional Metaphors Elicit Greater Real-Time Engagement Than Literal Paraphrases or Concrete Sentences." *Journal of Memory and Language* 121 (September 20, 2021): 104285.

Oh, Yongtaek, Christine Chesebrough, Brian Erickson, Fengqing Zhang, and John Kounios. "An Insight-Related Neural Reward Signal." *NeuroImage* 214 (2020): 116757.

Thibodeau, Paul H., and Lera Boroditsky. "Metaphors We Think With: The Role of Metaphor in Reasoning." *PloS ONE* 6, no. 2 (February 2011): e16782.

Thibodeau, Paul H., Rose K. Hendricks, and Lera Boroditsky. "How Linguistic Metaphor Scaffolds Reasoning." *Trends in Cognitive Sciences* 21, no. 11 (2017): 852–63.

Tik, Martin, Ronald Sladky, Caroline Di Bernardi Luft, David Willinger, André Hoffmann, Michael J. Banissy, Joydeep Bhattacharya, and Christian Windischberger. "Ultra-High-Field fMRI Insights on Insight: Neural Correlates of the Aha!-Moment." *Human Brain Mapping* 39, no. 8 (2018): 3241–52.

Chapter 7: Keep It Social

Dodell-Feder, David, Jorie Koster-Hale, Marina Bedny, and Rebecca Saxe. "fMRI Item Analysis in a Theory of Mind Task." *Neuroimage* 55, no. 2 (2011): 705–12.

Küfner, Albrecht C. P., Mitja D. Back, Steffen Nestler, and Boris Egloff. "Tell Me a Story and I Will Tell You Who You Are! Lens Model Analyses of Personality and Creative Writing." *Journal of Research in Personality* 44, no. 4 (2010): 427–35.

Mar, Raymond A. "The Neural Bases of Social Cognition and Story Comprehension." *Annual Review of Psychology* 62 (2011): 103–34.

Mayer, Richard E., Sherry Fennell, Lindsay Farmer, and Julie Campbell. "A Personalization Effect in Multimedia Learning: Students Learn Better When Words Are in Conversational Style Rather Than Formal Style." *Journal of Educational Psychology* 96, no. 2 (2004): 389–95.

Paxton, Richard J. "The Influence of Author Visibility on High School Students Solving a Historical Problem." *Cognition and Instruction* 20, no. 2 (2002): 197–248.

Tamir, Diana I., Andrew B. Bricker, David Dodell-Feder, and Jason P. Mitchell. "Reading Fiction and Reading Minds: The Role of Simulation in the Default Network." *Social Cognitive and Affective Neuroscience* 11, no. 2 (2016): 215–24.

Tamir, Diana I., and Brent L. Hughes. "Social Rewards: From Basic Social Building Blocks to Complex Social Behavior." *Perspectives on Psychological Science* 13, no. 6 (2018): 700–17.

Van Overwalle, Frank, Marijke Van Duynslaeger, Daphné Coomans, and Bert Timmermans. "Spontaneous Goal Inferences Are Often Inferred Faster Than Spontaneous Trait Inferences." *Journal of Experimental Social Psychology* 48, no. 1 (2012): 13–18.

Van Overwalle, Frank, and Marie Vandekerckhove. "Implicit and Explicit Social Mentalizing: Dual Processes Driven by a Shared Neural Network." *Frontiers in Human Neuroscience* 7 (September 2013): 560.

Chapter 8: Keep It Story-Driven

Bietti, Lucas M., Ottilie Tilston, and Adrian Bangerter. "Storytelling as Adaptive Collective Sensemaking." *Topics in Cognitive Science* 11, no. 4 (2019): 710–32.

Dehghani, Morteza, Reihane Boghrati, Kingson Man, Joe Hoover, Sarah I. Gimbel, Ashish Vaswani, Jason D. Zevin et al. "Decoding the Neural Representation of Story Meanings across Languages." *Human Brain Mapping* 38, no. 12 (September 20, 2017): 6096–106.

Green, Melanie C., and Timothy C. Brock. "The Role of Transportation in the Persuasiveness of Public Narratives." *Journal of Personality and Social Psychology* 79, no. 5 (2000): 701–21.

Isberner, Maj-Britt, Tobias Richter, Constanze Schreiner, Yanina Eisenbach, Christin Sommer, and Markus Appel. "Empowering Stories: Transportation into Narratives with Strong Protagonists Increases Self-Related Control Beliefs." *Discourse Processes* 56, no. 8 (2019): 575–98.

Kaplan, Jonas T., Sarah I. Gimbel, Morteza Dehghani, Mary Helen Immordino-Yang, Kenji Sagae, Jennifer D. Wong, Christine M. Tipper et al. "Processing Narratives Concerning Protected Values: A Cross-Cultural Investigation of Neural Correlates." *Cerebral Cortex* 27, no. 2 (January 7, 2017): 1428–38.

Küfner, Albrecht C. P., Mitja D. Back, Steffen Nestler, and Boris Egloff. "Tell Me a Story and I Will Tell You Who You Are! Lens Model Analyses of Personality and Creative Writing." *Journal of Research in Personality* 44, no. 4 (2010): 427–35.

Mar, Raymond A. "The Neural Bases of Social Cognition and Story Comprehension." *Annual Review of Psychology* 62 (2011): 103–34.

Mar, Raymond A, Jingyuan Li, Anh T. P. Nguyen, and Cindy P. Ta. "Memory and Comprehension of Narrative Versus Expository Texts: A Meta-Analysis." *Psychonomic Bulletin & Review* (January 6, 2021): 1–18.

Nguyen, Mai, Tamara Vanderwal, and Uri Hasson. "Shared Understanding of Narratives Is Correlated with Shared Neural Responses." *NeuroImage* 184 (September 12, 2019): 161–70.

Simony, Erez, Christopher J. Honey, Janice Chen, Olga Lositsky, Yaara Yeshurun, Ami Wiesel, and Uri Hasson. "Dynamic Reconfiguration of the Default Mode Network During Narrative Comprehension." *Nature Communications* 7, no. 1 (July 18, 2016): 1–13.

Smith, Daniel, Philip Schlaepfer, Katie Major, Mark Dyble, Abigail E. Page, James Thompson, Nikhil Chaudhary et al. "Cooperation and the Evolution of Hunter-Gatherer Storytelling." *Nature Communications* 8, no. 1 (2017): 1–9.

Tylén, Kristian, Peer Christensen, Andreas Roepstorff, Torben Lund, Svend Østergaard, and Merlin Donald. "Brains Striving for Coherence: Long-Term Cumulative Plot Formation in the Default Mode Network." *NeuroImage* 121 (July 26, 2015): 106–14.

Zadbood, Asieh, Janice Chen, Yuan Chang Leong, Kenneth A. Norman, and Uri Hasson. "How We Transmit Memories to Other Brains: Constructing Shared Neural Representations Via Communication." *Cerebral Cortex* 27, no. 10 (October 2017): 4988–5000.

NOTES

Introduction: Reward Your Reader

1. Adolfo M. García et al., "How Meaning Unfolds in Neural Time: Embodied Reactivations Can Precede Multimodal Semantic Effects During Language Processing," *NeuroImage* 197 (2019); and Rachel L. Moseley, Friedemann Pulvermüller, and Yury Shtyrov, "Sensorimotor Semantics on the Spot: Brain Activity Dissociates between Conceptual Categories within 150 Ms," *Scientific Reports* 3 (2013).
2. BrainFacts.org, "How Many Neurons Are in the Brain?" December 4, 2018, https://www.brainfacts.org/In-the-Lab/Meet-the-Researcher /2018/How-Many-Neurons-Are-In-The-Brain-120418.
3. Morten L. Kringelbach and Kent C. Berridge, "The Joyful Mind," *Scientific American* 307, no. 2 (2012).
4. Thanks to Jon Vara.
5. Beyond language, the hippocampus also stars in spatial memory and navigation.
6. For more on the concept of neuronal consensus, see Santa Fe Institute, "How Neurons Use Crowdsourcing to Make Decisions," *ScienceDaily*, June 6, 2017, https://www.sciencedaily.com/releases/2017/06 /170606135736.htm; and Bryan C. Daniels, Jessica C. Flack, David C. Krakauer, "Dual Coding Theory Explains Biphasic Collective Computation in Neural Decision-Making," *Frontiers in Neuroscience,* 2017; 11 DOI: 10.3389/fnins.2017.00313.
7. See also Berridge's commentary in Kent C. Berridge and Peter Dayan, "Liking," *Current Biology* 31, no. 24 (2021).
8. Kent C. Berridge and Morten L. Kringelbach, "Pleasure Systems in the Brain," *Neuron* 86, no. 3 (2015).
9. The reward circuit comprises a suite of components in the center of the brain. The components include, among others, the ventral tegmental area, nucleus accumbens, amygdala, caudate nucleus, hippocampus, cingulate cortex, hypothalamus, and substantia nigra. They play diverse roles, but they all work toward a simple end: to fashion a consensus to spur (or

suppress) motivation to act. While this happens, the reader's desire and pleasure wax and wane as the reward team discriminates between stimuli that are good, better, and best—or bad, worse, and worst. The circuit members are essentially always asking, "Is there a better offer?" If at any point a stimulus looks to have no value, the team members drop it and move on.

When your brain detects an interesting stimulus, neurons in two members of the circuit (the ventral tegmental area and substantia nigra) pump out dopamine. The dopamine streaks to the other members of the circuit. And streaks between the parts. And goes crossways. And heads back again. When the neurons in the circuit rate a stimulus as worthy—as if by acclamation or vote—the dopamine spurs the release of opioids and endocannabinoids naturally produced in the brain. These opioids, including morphine-like enkephalin, and endocannabinoids, including marijuana-like anandamide, produce pleasure in five brain "hotspots" embedded in the reward circuit.

When many of these hotspots get triggered as an ensemble—and they often appear to coordinate—they can give a person the feeling of bliss. The hotspots are anatomically small, no larger than the tip of your pinkie, but they have a big impact on how you feel. Other neurotransmitters— serotonin, orexin, glutamate, GABA—also operate in the reward circuit, mixed into the dopamine-opioid reward cocktail, but they are less prominent.

For a recent review of the operation of the hotspot network, see David Nguyen, Erin E. Naffziger, and Kent C. Berridge, "Positive Affect: Nature and Brain Bases of Liking and Wanting," *Current Opinion in Behavioral Sciences* 39 (2021). See also Morten L. Kringelbach and Kent C. Berridge, "The Affective Core of Emotion: Linking Pleasure, Subjective Well-Being, and Optimal Metastability in the Brain," *Emotion Review* 9, no. 3 (2017): 191–99.

10. For a current review of the role of dopamine in reward, see Kelly M. J. Diederen and Paul C. Fletcher, "Dopamine, Prediction Error and Beyond," *The Neuroscientist* 27, no. 1 (2021). For another explanation of the wanting-liking-learning phases in the reward circuit, see Kent C. Berridge, "Evolving Concepts of Emotion and Motivation," *Frontiers in Psychology* 9 (2018).

11. Lewis Thomas, *Lives of a Cell* (New York: Penguin, 1978).

12. Eugen Wassiliwizky et al., "The Emotional Power of Poetry: Neural Circuitry, Psychophysiology and Compositional Principles," *Social Cognitive and Affective Neuroscience* 12, no. 8 (2017).

13. Inferred from Michael Gazzaniga, Richard Ivry, and George Mangun, *Cognitive Neuroscience* (New York: W. W. Norton, 2019): 105; and Wikipedia, s.v. "Functional magnetic resonance imaging," last modified August

18, 2022, 14:41, https://en.wikipedia.org/wiki/Functional_magnetic_resonance_imaging.

14. Gazzaniga et al., *Cognitive Neuroscience*, 106.

15. The EEG locations are inexact. They could be off by a centimeter.

16. Stephen R. Anderson, "How Many Languages Are There in the World?" in *Linguistic Society of America* brochure series (Linguistic Society of America, 2010), https://www.linguisticsociety.org/sites/default/fileshow-many-languages.pdf.

17. Fatma Deniz et al., "The Representation of Semantic Information across Human Cerebral Cortex During Listening Versus Reading Is Invariant to Stimulus Modality," *Journal of Neuroscience* 39, no. 39 (2019).

18. Christopher S. von Bartheld, Jami Bahney, and Suzana Herculano-Houzel, "The Search for True Numbers of Neurons and Glial Cells in the Human Brain: A Review of 150 Years of Cell Counting," *Journal of Comparative Neurology* 524, no. 18 (December 15, 2016), https://www.ncbi.nlm.nih.gov/pmc/articles/PMC5063692/pdf/nihms799882.pdf.

Chapter 1: Keep It Simple

1. Ernest Hemingway, *A Moveable Feast* (New York: Scribner, 1964).

2. John Steinbeck, *Travels with Charley* (New York: Penguin, 1980).

3. Daniel M. Oppenheimer, "Consequences of Erudite Vernacular Utilized Irrespective of Necessity: Problems with Using Long Words Needlessly," *Applied Cognitive Psychology: The Official Journal of the Society for Applied Research in Memory and Cognition* 20, no. 2 (2006).

4. Multiple studies show that more complex reading recruits more brain circuits. See Marcel Adam Just, Patricia A. Carpenter, Timothy A. Keller, William F. Eddy, and Keith R. Thulborn, "Brain Activation Modulated by Sentence Comprehension," *Science* 274 (October 4, 1996): 114–16; or more recently, Angela D. Friederici, Christian J. Fiebach, Matthias Schlesewsky, Ina D. Bornkessel, and D. Yves von Cramon, "Processing Linguistic Complexity and Grammaticality in the Left Frontal Cortex," *Cerebral Cortex* 16, no. 12 (December 1, 2006): 1709–1717.

5. Jan R. Landwehr and Lisa Eckmann, "The Nature of Processing Fluency: Amplification Versus Hedonic Marking," *Journal of Experimental Social Psychology* 90 (2020). Landwehr and Echmann confirm that "fluent processing is a hedonically positive experience that triggers positive affect." For a literature review on the positive effect of processing fluency, particularly as it affects writing in healthcare, see Tsuyoshi Okuhara et al., "Designing Persuasive Health Materials Using Processing Fluency: A Literature Review," *BMC Research Notes* 10, no. 1 (2017). Other research shows that more coherent stories stimulate more activity in the reward circuit. See Eleanor A. Maguire, Christopher D. Frith, and

R. G. M. Morris, "The Functional Neuroanatomy of Comprehension and Memory: The Importance of Prior Knowledge," *Brain* 122, no. 10 (1999). In this case, the 13 subjects in the experiments *listened* to the stories for ninety seconds while undergoing a positron emission tomography (PET) scan. Overall, the researchers found that the easier a story is to understand, the more it lights up the medial ventral orbitofrontal cortex, a part of the brain responsible for "feeling" pleasure.

6. A variety of studies finds that people like easy-to-process content. The brain doesn't have to work so hard. See, for example, Just et al., "Brain Activation Modulated by Sentence Comprehension," 114–16.

7. Author interview with Piotr Winkielman, University of California, San Diego, April 4, 2022. Winkielman noted in the interview that the so-called hedonic benefits from simplicity go only so far. Many other factors, such as surprise, awe, and profundity matter, too. For more detail on his work with the aesthetic pleasure from processing fluency, see Piotr Winkielman et al., "The Hedonic Marking of Processing Fluency: Implications for Evaluative Judgment," *The Psychology of Evaluation: Affective Processes in Cognition and Emotion* 189 (2003). See also Troy Chenier and Piotr Winkielman, "The Origins of Aesthetic Pleasure: Processing Fluency and Affect in Judgment, Body, and the Brain," in *Neuroaesthetics* (London: Routledge, 2009).

8. Mark Jung-Beeman, "Bilateral Brain Processes for Comprehending Natural Language," *Trends in Cognitive Sciences* 9, no. 11 (2005).

9. Just et al., "Brain Activation Modulated by Sentence Comprehension," 114–16.

10. Angela D. Friederici et al., "Processing Linguistic Complexity and Grammaticality in the Left Frontal Cortex," *Cerebral Cortex* 16, no. 12 (2006). The experiment was done in German, but research shows the brain works the same across languages.

11. James Clear, *Atomic Habits* (New York: Avery (Penguin), 2018), chapter 1.

12. Kurt Vonnegut, *Dispatch from a Man Without a Country* (London: Bloomsbury, 2005).

13. George A. Miller, "The Magical Number Seven, Plus or Minus Two: Some Limits on our Capacity for Processing Information," *Psychological Review* 63 (1956): 81–97. Note that the "magic number" is not always seven, but Miller simplified his point to a general rule. Wikipedia, s.v. "The Magical Number Seven, Plus or Minus Two," last modified April 15, 2022, 00:55, http://en.wikipedia.org/wiki/The_Magical_Number _Seven,_Plus_or_Minus_Two.

14. As with George Miller's research, research on chunking has not *proven* that four is the limit, but again, many scientists have settled on four as roughly correct. See the article and commentary in Nelson Cowan, "The Magical Number 4 in Short-Term Memory: A Reconsideration of

Mental Storage Capacity," *Behavioral and Brain Sciences*. 24, no. 1 (2001): 87–114, discussion 114–85. For a summary of the wealth of research on memory and processing stimulated by Miller, see Wikipedia, s.v. "The Magical Number Seven, Plus or Minus Two."

15. For a summary of the history and science behind this idea, see Nick Chater, "The Search for Simplicity: A Fundamental Cognitive Principle?" *The Quarterly Journal of Experimental Psychology* 52A, no. 2 (1999): 273–302. Or for another, more recent view on the "simplicity principle," see Jacob Feldman, "The Simplicity Principle in Perception and Cognition," *Wiley Interdisciplinary Reviews: Cognitive Science* 7, no. 5 (2016).

16. Again, see Chater, "The Search for Simplicity," 277; and Feldman, "The Simplicity Principle in Perception and Cognition."

17. For a longer explanation of Kolmogorov's thinking, see Nick Chater, "Simplicity and the Mind," *Psychologist* (November 1997): 294–95; and Chater, "The Search for Simplicity" 273–302.

18. Albert E. N. Gray, "The Common Denominator of Success," speech originally delivered to the National Association of Life Underwriters at their annual convention in 1940. The four common habits: prospecting habits, calling habits, selling habits, and working habits, all driven by a practical purpose in life. See the transcript of this speech on the website of James Clear, https://jamesclear.com/great-speeches/the-common -denominator-of-success-by-albert-e-n-gray.

19. Mark Twain, letter to D. W. Bowser, 20 March 1880, http://www -twainquotes.com/Writing.html.

20. Jonah Berger, Wendy W. Moe, and David Schweidel, "What Leads to Longer Reads? Psychological Drivers of Reading Online Content," *ACR North American Advances* (2019).

21. Tsuyoshi Okuhara et al., "Influence of High Versus Low Readability Level of Written Health Information on Self-Efficacy: A Randomized Controlled Study of the Processing Fluency Effect," *Health Psychology Open* 7, no. 1 (2020). This study was done in Japanese.

22. Hillary C. Shulman et al., "The Effects of Jargon on Processing Fluency, Self-Perceptions, and Scientific Engagement," *Journal of Language and Social Psychology* 39, no. 5–6 (2020).

23. Byoung-Hyoun Hwang and Hugh Hoikwang Kim, "It Pays to Write Well," *Journal of Financial Economics* 124, no. 2 (2017). Hwang and Kim studied closed-end investment companies, which invest in other companies. By studying just these firms, they could calculate the difference between the publicly traded value of their stock and the sum of the publicly traded values of company holdings underlying their stock. In an efficient market, with "perfect" information, the values would be the same. But if investors can't easily read company reports, prices get distorted. A host of studies of corporate finance suggests that readability

creates value by raising stock prices, reducing debt costs, lowering audit costs, and more. See for example, Hongkang Xu, Trung H Pham, and Mai Dao, "Annual Report Readability and Trade Credit," *Review of Accounting and Finance* 19, no. 3 (2020); Arvid O. I. Hoffmann and Stefanie Kleimeier, "Financial Disclosure Readability and Innovative Firms' Cost of Debt," *International Review of Finance* 21, no. 2 (2021); Hatem Rjiba et al., "Annual Report Readability and the Cost of Equity Capital," *Journal of Corporate Finance* 67 (2021).

24. U.S. Securities and Exchange Commission, *A Plain English Handbook* (Washington, D.C.: U.S. Securities and Exchange Commission, 1998). See https://www.sec.gov/pdf/handbook.pdf. Note that more recently the U.S. Congress extended the plain-writing mandate. The Plain Writing Act was signed into law in 2010 (Public Law 111–274). It applies to all U.S. agencies, including the SEC.

25. Attributed to mystic Meister Eckhart, 1260–1327:
    The soul grows by subtraction, not addition . . .
    Thou must be emptied of what wherewith thou art
    full, that thou may be filled with that whereof thou
    art empty . . . Only those who dare to let go can
    dare to re-enter.

26. Magdalena Formanowicz et al., "'Make It Happen!': Verbs as Markers of Agency Increase Message Effectiveness," *Social Psychology* 52, no. 5 (2021).

27. Darrell Huff, *How to Lie with Statistics* (New York: W. W. Norton, 1982), 74.

28. Roger Fisher, William Ury, and Bruce Patton, *Getting to Yes* (Boston: Houghton Mifflin, 1981), xi.

29. Dustin Poppendieck and Mengyan Gong, "Measurement of Airborne Emissions from Extinguished Cigarettes: Final Report" (Washington, D.C: National Institute for Standards and Technology, December 2019), 2, https://www.govinfo.gov/content/pkg/GOVPUB -C13-d47c61d9557911e8778cad7102c3d74c/pdf/GOVPUB-C13 -d47c61d9557911e8778cad7102c3d74c.pdf.

30. Interview with Warren Buffett, *Adam Smith's Money World: How to Pick Stocks & Get Rich,* PBS (1985): https://www.youtube.com/watch?v =vCpT-UmVf3g.

31. Attributed to Duke Ellington. Another version credited to Ellington: "Life has two rules: number 1, never quit! Number 2, always remember rule number one."

32. Virginia Woolf, *A Room of One's Own,* 1929. *A Room of One's Own* was an essay based on Woolf's lectures in 1928. A fuller passage: "Women have served all these centuries as looking-glasses possessing the magic and delicious power of reflecting the figure of man at twice its natural

size. . . . How is he to go on giving judgement, civilizing natives, making laws, writing books, dressing up and speechifying at banquets, unless he can see himself at breakfast and at dinner at least twice the size he really is? So I reflected, crumbling my bread and stirring my coffee and now and again looking at the people in the street. The looking-glass vision is of supreme importance because it charges the vitality; it stimulates the nervous system. Take it away and man may die, like the drug fiend deprived of his cocaine."

33. Charles Darwin, *The Origin of Species* (London: John Murray, 1859). Available online at https://archive.org/stream/originofspecies00darwuoft /originofspecies00darwuoft_djvu.txt.

34. Darwin passage after cross-outs:

Until recently the great majority of naturalists believed that species were immutable productions, separately created. Some naturalists, on the other hand, have believed that species undergo modification, and existing forms of life are descendants of pre-existing forms. The first author who treated [the subject] in a scientific spirit was Buffon. But as he does not enter on the causes or means of the transformation of species, I need not here enter on details. (73 words)

Chapter 2: Keep It Specific

1. Brian Wansink, James Painter, and Koert Van Ittersum, "Descriptive Menu Labels' Effect on Sales," *Cornell Hotel and Restaurant Administration Quarterly* 42, no. 6 (2001).

2. Tracy Roxbury, Katie McMahon, and David A. Copland, "An fMRI Study of Concreteness Effects in Spoken Word Recognition," *Behavioral and Brain Functions* 10, no. 1 (2014).

3. David Brooks, *The Road to Character* (New York: Random House, 2016), 5.

4. Vittorio Gallese and George Lakoff, "The Brain's Concepts: The Role of the Sensory-Motor System in Conceptual Knowledge," *Cognitive Neuropsychology* 22, no. 3–4 (2005).

5. Alfonso Barrós-Loscertales et al., "Reading Salt Activates Gustatory Brain Regions: fMRI Evidence for Semantic Grounding in a Novel Sensory Modality," *Cerebral Cortex* 22, no. 11 (2012). This study reaffirmed findings in an earlier one: Dana M. Small et al., "The Role of the Human Orbitofrontal Cortex in Taste and Flavor Processing," *Annals of the New York Academy of Sciences* 1121, no. 1 (2007).

6. Markus Kiefer and Marcel Harpaintner, "Varieties of Abstract Concepts and Their Grounding in Perception or Action," *Open Psychology* 2, no. 1 (2020).

7. Lyrics from one version of "Old Chisholm Trail," John Lomax, *Cowboy Songs and Other Frontier Ballads,* 1910.
8. Author interview with Arthur Glenberg, May 10, 2022. See also Arthur M. Glenberg, "Few Believe the World Is Flat: How Embodiment Is Changing the Scientific Understanding of Cognition," *Canadian Journal of Experimental Psychology/Revue Canadienne de Psychologie Expérimentale* 69, no. 2 (2015).
9. Author interview with Benjamin Bergen, April 29, 2022.
10. Roxbury, McMahon, and Copland, "An fMRI Study of Concreteness Effects in Spoken Word Recognition." As with other experiments with readers, the brain acts in the same way across languages. See, for example, the concreteness effect in Chinese: Dawei Wei and Margaret Gillon-Dowens, "Written-Word Concreteness Effects in Non-Attend Conditions: Evidence from Mismatch Responses and Cortical Oscillations," *Frontiers in Psychology* 9 (2018).
11. Recent experiments suggest that abstract words get less extensive coding, leaving more of the burden of word processing on the Wernicke's and nearby areas. See Diana Kurmakaeva et al., "Acquisition of Concrete and Abstract Words Is Modulated by tDCS of Wernicke's Area," *Scientific Reports* 11, no. 1 (2021).
12. Paula J. Schwanenflugel, Carolyn Akin, and Wei-Ming Luh, "Context Availability and the Recall of Abstract and Concrete Words," *Memory & Cognition* 20, no. 1 (1992); and Klaus Fliessbach et al., "The Effect of Word Concreteness on Recognition Memory," *NeuroImage* 32, no. 3 (2006).
13. Wessel O. Van Dam, Shirley-Ann Rueschemeyer, and Harold Bekkering, "How Specifically Are Action Verbs Represented in the Neural Motor System: An fMRI Study," *Neuroimage* 53, no. 4 (2010).
14. For a recent meta-analysis of the regions active in concrete word processing, with emphasis on visual areas, see Madalina Bucur and Costanza Papagno, "The Anatomical Correlates of Abstract and Concrete Words: A Meta-Analytical Review of Whole-Brain Imaging Studies," *Scientific Reports* 11 (2021).
15. Grant Packard and Jonah Berger, "How Concrete Language Shapes Customer Satisfaction," *Journal of Consumer Research* 47, no. 5 (2021).
16. Rolf A. Zwaan, Robert A. Stanfield, and Richard H. Yaxley, "Language Comprehenders Mentally Represent the Shapes of Objects," *Psychological Science* 13, no. 2 (2002).
17. For example, in one experiment, with people reading action verbs, researchers confirmed that the brain's motor strip fires. See García et al., "How Meaning Unfolds in Neural Time: Embodied Reactivations Can Precede Multimodal Semantic Effects During Language Processing." See also Moseley, Pulvermüller, and Shtyrov, "Sensorimotor Semantics

on the Spot: Brain Activity Dissociates between Conceptual Categories within 150 Ms."

18. Julio González et al., "Reading Cinnamon Activates Olfactory Brain Regions," *NeuroImage* 32, no. 2 (2006).

19. William Deresiewicz, "Solitude and Leadership," *The American Scholar,* 1 March 2010. Text of lecture delivered at the United States Military Academy at West Point, October 2009. Available online at https:// theamericanscholar.org/solitude-and-leadership/.

20. J. K. Rowling, Commencement Speech to Harvard University, 5 June 2008. Available online at https://www.youtube.com/watch?v =nkREt4ZB-ck.

21. Marco Tettamanti et al., "Listening to Action-Related Sentences Activates Fronto-Parietal Motor Circuits," *Journal of Cognitive Neuroscience* 17, no. 2 (2005). For more recent research in this area, see Nikola Vukovic et al., "Primary Motor Cortex Functionally Contributes to Language Comprehension: An Online rTMS Study," *Neuropsychologia* 96 (2017).

22. Van Dam, Rueschemeyer, and Bekkering, "How Specifically Are Action Verbs Represented in the Neural Motor System: An fMRI Study."

23. Simon Lacey, Randall Stilla, and Krish Sathian, "Metaphorically Feeling: Comprehending Textural Metaphors Activates Somatosensory Cortex," *Brain and Language* 120, no. 3 (2012).

24. "The Emperor's New Clothes," The Hans Christian Andersen Centre, last modified August 11, 2022, https://andersen.sdu.dk/vaerk/hersholt /TheEmperorsNewClothes_e.html.

25. The brain regions under study included the anterior inferior parietal and posterior inferior temporal areas. See Rutvik H. Desai et al., "Toward Semantics in the Wild: Activation to Manipulable Nouns in Naturalistic Reading," *Journal of Neuroscience* 36, no. 14 (2016).

26. Michael J. Spivey et al., "Eye Movements During Comprehension of Spoken Scene Descriptions" (paper presented at the Proceedings of the Twenty-Second Annual Conference of the Cognitive Science Society, 2000). See also Benjamin K. Bergen et al., "Spatial and Linguistic Aspects of Visual Imagery in Sentence Comprehension," *Cognitive Science* 31, no. 5 (2007).

27. Laura J. Speed and Gabriella Vigliocco, "Eye Movements Reveal the Dynamic Simulation of Speed in Language," *Cognitive Science* 38, no. 2 (2014).

28. Germán Gálvez-García et al., "Muscle Activation in Semantic Processing: An Electromyography Approach," *Biological Psychology* 152 (2020).

29. Kiefer and Harpaintner, "Varieties of Abstract Concepts and Their Grounding in Perception or Action."

30. Author interview with Arthur Glenberg, May 10, 2022.

31. John F. Stins et al., "Words That Move Us. The Effects of Sentences on Body Sway," *Advances in Cognitive Psychology* 13, no. 2 (2017).

32. For recent thinking on simulation of concepts, see Leonardo Fernandino et al., "Decoding the Information Structure Underlying the Neural Representation of Concepts," *Proceedings of the National Academy of Sciences* 119, no. 6 (2022).

33. Felix R. Dreyer and Friedemann Pulvermüller, "Abstract Semantics in the Motor System? An Event-Related fMRI Study on Passive Reading of Semantic Word Categories Carrying Abstract Emotional and Mental Meaning," *Cortex* 100 (2018).

34. Data cited in Marcel Harpaintner et al., "The Grounding of Abstract Concepts in the Motor and Visual System: An fMRI Study," *Cortex* 124 (November 13, 2020): 1–22.

35. Benjamin K. Bergen, *Louder Than Words* (New York: Basic Books, 2012), 59.

36. Mark Twain, Essay on William Dean Howells, 1906.

37. George Orwell, "Politics and the English Language," 1946.

38. Jeff Bezos, "2018 Letter to Shareholders," April 11, 2019, Amazon, https://www.aboutamazon.com/news/company-news/2018-letter-to-shareholders.

39. W. E. B. Du Bois. *The Souls of Black Folk* (Chicago: A. C. McClurg, 1903).

40. Wikiquote, s.v. "Crowfoot," last modified May 14, 2019, 17:44, https://en.wikiquote.org/wiki/Crowfoot.

41. Steven Pinker, *The Sense of Style* (New York: Penguin, 2014) 67.

42. Zane Grey, *The Last of the Plainsmen* (London: Outing Publishing, 1908).

43. Siddhartha Mukherjee, *The Emperor of All Maladies: A Biography of Cancer.* (New York: Scribner, 2011).

44. Marc Reisner, *Cadillac Desert* (New York: Viking Penguin, 1986).

Chapter 3: Keep It Surprising

1. For a recent summary of how the brain works as a prediction engine, see J. Benjamin Hutchinson and Lisa Feldman Barrett, "The Power of Predictions: An Emerging Paradigm for Psychological Research," *Current Directions in Psychological Science* 28, no. 3 (2019).

2. John McPhee, "The Search for Marvin Gardens," *The New Yorker,* September 9, 1972, https://www.newyorker.com/magazine/1972/09/09/the-search-for-marvin-gardens.

3. Ed Yong, *I Contain Multitudes* (New York: HarperCollins, 2016), 17.

4. Joan Didion, "Why I Write," *The New York Times Book Review,* December 1976.

5. Description in display case, Little Bighorn Battlefield National Monument museum, Crow Agency, Montana.

6. Corinna E. Bonhage et al., "Combined Eye Tracking and fMRI Reveals Neural Basis of Linguistic Predictions During Sentence Comprehen-

sion," *Cortex* 68 (2015); and Nathaniel J. Smith and Roger Levy, "The Effect of Word Predictability on Reading Time Is Logarithmic," *Cognition* 128, no. 3 (2013).

7. A body of research links novelty and surprise to reward. See for example, Ruth M. Krebs et al., "Novelty Increases the Mesolimbic Functional Connectivity of the Substantia Nigra/Ventral Tegmental Area (SN/VTA) During Reward Anticipation: Evidence from High-Resolution fMRI," *Neuroimage* 58, no. 2 (2011). See also Andrew R. Tapper and Susanna Molas, "Midbrain Circuits of Novelty Processing," *Neurobiology of Learning and Memory* 176 (2020). For effects of unpredictability unrelated to language, see, for example, Gregory S. Berns et al., "Predictability Modulates Human Brain Response to Reward," *Journal of Neuroscience* 21, no. 8 (2001).

8. Novelty increases attention, arousal, motivation, and learning, although different kinds of novelty may spur each one and not all at the same time. See J. Schomaker and M. Meeter, "Short- and Long-Lasting Consequences of Novelty, Deviance and Surprise on Brain and Cognition," *Neuroscience & Biobehavioral Reviews* 55 (2015).

9. For an in-depth look at dopamine circulation in response to surprise in both humans and rodents, see Tapper and Molas, "Midbrain Circuits of Novelty Processing." See also Diederen and Fletcher, "Dopamine, Prediction Error and Beyond."

10. Alexandros Kafkas and Daniela Montaldi, "Two Separate, but Interacting, Neural Systems for Familiarity and Novelty Detection: A Dual-Route Mechanism," *Hippocampus* 24, no. 5 (2014). See also Felipe Fredes and Ryuichi Shigemoto, "The Role of Hippocampal Mossy Cells in Novelty Detection," *Neurobiology of Learning and Memory* (2021). The research on novelty and surprise suggests the two are not the same and are handled differently in the brain. A number of researchers find the anterior cingulate cortex (ACC), insula, and striatum handle surprise. See, for example, Elsa Fouragnan, Chris Retzler, and Marios G. Philiastides, "Separate Neural Representations of Prediction Error Valence and Surprise: Evidence from an fMRI Meta-Analysis," *Human Brain Mapping* 39, no. 7 (2018). I have not tried to distinguish the neural correlates of novelty and surprise owing to the complexity and ongoing research. It appears that the hippocampus handles novelty, or stimuli never before experienced, and the ACC, insula, and striatum handle surprise, or stimuli never before detected in the particular context. In any case, both novelty and surprise activate what scientists call the prediction error and reward prediction error circuits (PE and RPE). The activations appear in parallel and are almost certainly integrated.

11. Schomaker and Meeter, "Short- and Long-Lasting Consequences of Novelty, Deviance and Surprise on Brain and Cognition" (2015); Alex

Kafkas and Daniela Montaldi, "How Do Memory Systems Detect and Respond to Novelty?" *Neuroscience Letters* 680 (2018); and Nico Bunzeck et al., "Contextual Interaction between Novelty and Reward Processing within the Mesolimbic System," *Human Brain Mapping* 33, no. 6 (2012).

12. Berns et al., "Predictability Modulates Human Brain Response to Reward."

13. That it's subliminal is my speculation, based on a wealth of research that shows that people do process and act on stimuli (like brief flashes of photos) that they don't consciously detect.

14. Jean-Louis Dessalles, "Have You Anything Unexpected to Say? The Human Propensity to Communicate Surprise and Its Role in the Emergence of Language" (paper presented at the Evolution of Language—Proceedings of the Eighth International Conference, Utrecht, 2010). This study was in French, with 101 participants.

15. For a discussion in this area, see also Alessandra Zarcone et al., "Salience and Attention in Surprisal-Based Accounts of Language Processing," *Frontiers in Psychology* 7 (2016).

16. For a discussion of the Goldilocks idea, see Andy Clark, "A Nice Surprise? Predictive Processing and the Active Pursuit of Novelty," *Phenomenology and the Cognitive Sciences* 17, no. 3 (2018).

17. Katherine A. DeLong, Thomas P. Urbach, and Marta Kutas, "Probabilistic Word Pre-Activation During Language Comprehension Inferred from Electrical Brain Activity," *Nature Neuroscience* 8, no. 8 (2005). See also the replication of this study: Thomas P. Urbach et al., "An Exploratory Data Analysis of Word Form Prediction During Word-by-Word Reading," *Proceedings of the National Academy of Sciences* 117, no. 34 (2020).

18. Corinna Bonhage and colleagues took another approach to show word prediction. They took fMRI images to confirm it. They asked people to read sentences cut off just before the end, pausing five seconds before the last word. People didn't know why—they just kept waiting after the pause. When the final word came up, they were told they should push a button to show if the sentence made sense or if it did not.

The sentences were written so that people could easily infer if the word about to appear on the screen was a noun or verb. If the word was a verb, it would appear in the top right of the screen, and if a noun, the bottom right.

You can see what Bonhage and her colleagues were up to. If readers were predicting, they would flash their gaze to either the top right or bottom right before the word appeared, depending on whether it should be a noun or verb.

And that's what readers did. With a machine tracking eye movement, Bonhage's team showed that people consistently flashed their eyes to the part of the screen that would predict the right part of speech. A swath

NOTES 217

of regions dedicated to language processing meanwhile lit up, as well as
parts like the hippocampus.

See Corinna E. Bonhage, Jutta L. Mueller, Angela D. Friederici, and
Christian J. Fiebach, "Combined Eye Tracking and fMRI Reveals Neu-
ral Basis of Linguistic Predictions During Sentence Comprehension,"
Cortex 68 (2015): 33–47.

19. Luigi Grisoni, Tally McCormick Miller, and Friedemann Pulvermüller,
"Neural Correlates of Semantic Prediction and Resolution in Sentence
Processing," *Journal of Neuroscience* 37, no. 18 (2017).

20. Judith Gerten and Sascha Topolinski, "Shades of Surprise: Assessing Surprise as a Function of Degree of Deviance and Expectation Constraints,"
Cognition 192 (2019).

21. Jonah Berger and Katherine L. Milkman, "What Makes Online Content
Viral?," *Journal of Marketing Research* 49, no. 2 (2012).

22. Ahmed Al-Rawi, "Viral News on Social Media," *Digital Journalism* 7, no.
1 (2019).

23. Hannah Rohde, Richard Futrell, and Christopher G. Lucas, "What's
New? A Comprehension Bias in Favor of Informativity," *Cognition* 209
(2021).

24. Schomaker and Meeter, "Short- and Long-Lasting Consequences of Novelty, Deviance and Surprise on Brain and Cognition" (2015); see page
274. See also Darya Frank and Alex Kafkas, "Expectation-Driven Novelty Effects in Episodic Memory," *Neurobiology of Learning and Memory* 183
(2021). The memory-enhancement effect of novelty depends on the nature of the novelty; for example, novel contexts versus novel stimuli.

25. Jörn Alexander Quent, Richard N. Henson, and Andrea Greve. "A Predictive Account of How Novelty Influences Declarative Memory." *Neurobiology of Learning and Memory* 179 (January 18, 2021): 107382.

26. J. Poppenk et al., "Why Is the Meaning of a Sentence Better Remem-
bered Than Its Form? An fMRI Study on the Role of Novelty-Encoding
Processes," *Hippocampus* 18, no. 9 (2008).

27. Barbara Mellers et al., "Surprise: A Belief or an Emotion?," in *Progress in
Brain Research*, ed. V. S. Chandrasekhar Pammi and Narayanan Srinivasan
(Amsterdam: Elsevier, 2013).

28. John McPhee, *Basin and Range* (New York: Farrar, Straus and Giroux,
1982). Kindle.

29. Sheri Fink, *Five Days at Memorial* (New York, Crown, 2016), 11.

30. As Samuel Johnson said, "In this work are exhibited, in a very high degree, the two most engaging powers of an author. New things are made
familiar, and familiar things are made new." Samuel Johnson, "The Works
of Samuel Johnson, LL.D.: Together with His Life, and Notes on His
Lives of the Poets, by Sir John Hawkins, Knt. In Eleven Volumes . . ."
(1787), 122, https://www.azquotes.com/quote/1127328.

31. Christopher Hitchens, *Mortality* (New York: Twelve, 2012), 1.

32. Rutvik H. Desai et al., "A Piece of the Action: Modulation of Sensory-Motor Regions by Action Idioms and Metaphors," *NeuroImage* 83 (2013).

33. Thanks to Emily Archer.

34. Carl Zimmer, *Life's Edge* (New York: Dutton, 2021), xviii.

35. James Baldwin, *Notes of a Native Son,* (Boston: Beacon Press, 1955).

36. T. Colin Campbell and Thomas M. Campbell, *The China Study* (Dallas: BenBella Books, 2016), 111.

37. Suzanne Simard, *Finding the Mother Tree* (New York: Knopf, 2021), 6.

38. Jon Franklin, *The Wolf in the Parlor,* (New York: Henry Holt, 2009), 27.

39. Seth Godin, *The Dip* (New York: Portfolio, 2007), 4.

40. L. Frank Baum, *The Wonderful Wizard of Oz* (Chicago: George M. Hill, 1900).

41. Scientists have shown that the endings of poetry can be particularly rewarding, with marked action sparked in the reward circuit. People experience chills at the ends of lines, stanzas, and entire poems. See Wassiliwizky et al., "The Emotional Power of Poetry: Neural Circuitry, Psychophysiology and Compositional Principles" (2017).

42. Chris Impey, "The Scariest Things in the Universe are Black Holes—And Here Are 3 Reasons," *The Conversation,* 30 October 2020, https://theconversation.com/the-scariest-things-in-the-universe-are-black-holes-and-here-are-3-reasons-148615.

43. Victor Hugo, *Les Misérables* (New York: Bigelow, Smith & Company, ca 1862) volume IV (St. Denis), book VII, chapter 1, 184. See full text online: https://holybooks-lichtenbergpress.netdna-ssl.com/wp-content/uploads/Les-miserables-part-4.

44. William Jacob Holland, *The Moth Book: A Popular Guide to the Knowledge of the Moths of North America,* (New York: Doubleday, Page, & Company, 1903), epilogue.

Chapter 4: Keep It Stirring

1. Hugh Knickerbocker, Rebecca L. Johnson, and Jeanette Altarriba, "Emotion Effects During Reading: Influence of an Emotion Target Word on Eye Movements and Processing," *Cognition and Emotion* 29, no. 5 (2015). Note that the speed of emotion processing depends on how scientists are measuring it. Some scientists cite evidence of activation in as little as 50 milliseconds. But the "arousal" of emotions (as opposed to the "valence") seems to undergo processing in well under 200 milliseconds.

2. Francesca M. M. Citron, "Neural Correlates of Written Emotion Word Processing: A Review of Recent Electrophysiological and Hemodynamic Neuroimaging Studies," *Brain and Language* 122, no. 3 (2012). See

also Graham G. Scott, Patrick J. O'Donnell, and Sara C. Sereno, "Emotion Words Affect Eye Fixations During Reading," *Journal of Experimental Psychology: Learning, Memory, and Cognition* 38, no. 3 (2012): 783.

3. Citron, "Neural Correlates of Written Emotion Word Processing."

4. Author interview with Francesca Citron, Lancaster University (UK), April 27, 2022.

5. Antonio Damasio and Gil B. Carvalho, "The Nature of Feelings: Evolutionary and Neurobiological Origins," *Nature Reviews Neuroscience* 14, no. 2 (2013). For a more general view of the role of emotion during the evolution of the brain, see Leda Cosmides and John Tooby, "Evolutionary Psychology and the Emotions," in *Handbook of Emotions*, ed. M. Lewis and J. M. Haviland-Jones (New York: Guilford, 2000).

6. W. Chan Kim and Renée Mauborgne, *Blue Ocean Strategy* (Boston: Harvard Business School Publishing, 2015).

7. Carlos Eire, *Waiting for Snow in Havana: Confessions of a Cuban Boy* (New York: Free Press, 2004), 224.

8. For an excellent summary of grounded cognition spurred by emotional words, see Piotr Winkielman, Seana Coulson, and Paula Niedenthal, "Dynamic Grounding of Emotion Concepts," *Philosophical Transactions of the Royal Society B: Biological Sciences* 373, no. 1752 (2018).

9. Arthur M. Jacobs et al., "10 Years of BAWLing into Affective and Aesthetic Processes in Reading: What Are the Echoes?," *Frontiers in Psychology* 6 (2015).

10. Morten L. Kringelbach and Kent C. Berridge, "The Affective Core of Emotion: Linking Pleasure, Subjective Well-Being, and Optimal Metastability in the Brain," *Emotion Review* 9, no. 3 (2017).

11. As one example, see Francesca M. M. Citron et al., "Idiomatic Expressions Evoke Stronger Emotional Responses in the Brain Than Literal Sentences," *Neuropsychologia* 131 (2019).

12. Karim S. Kassam et al., "Identifying Emotions on the Basis of Neural Activation," *PloS ONE* 8, no. 6 (2013).

13. Arash Aryani et al., "Why 'Piss' Is Ruder Than 'Pee'? The Role of Sound in Affective Meaning Making," *PloS ONE* 31, no. 8 (2018).

14. Michael Gazzaniga, Richard Ivry, and George Mangun, *Cognitive Neuroscience: The Biology of the Mind* (New York: W. W. Norton, 2019) 455.

15. Rajendra D. Badgaiyan, "Dopamine Is Released in the Striatum During Human Emotional Processing," *Neuroreport* 21, no. 18 (2010).

16. Positive stories engaged more of the nucleus accumbens and negative ones more of the amygdala. Costa's team concluded that the amygdala, nucleus accumbens, and prefrontal cortex all play a role in the reward circuit. Vincent D. Costa et al., "Emotional Imagery: Assessing Pleasure and Arousal in the Brain's Reward Circuitry," *Human Brain Mapping* 31, no. 9 (2010).

17. Wrote the researchers: "a deliberate choice for death, violence or harm is associated with activation in the striatum (NAcc [nucleus accumbens], caudate, and putamen)"—three core components of the brain's reward circuitry. Suzanne Oosterwijk et al., "Choosing to View Morbid Information Involves Reward Circuitry," *Scientific Reports* 10, no. 1 (2020).

18. In case you're wondering, this partly explains the neurology of addiction, but that's another story, one that has spawned a wealth of research on the reward circuit.

19. Edita Fino et al., "Enjoying vs. Smiling: Facial Muscular Activation in Response to Emotional Language," *Biological Psychology* 118 (2016).

20. Alessandra Vergallito et al., "Somatic and Visceral Effects of Word Valence, Arousal and Concreteness in a Continuum Lexical Space," *Scientific Reports* 9, no. 1 (2019).

21. David A. Havas, Arthur M. Glenberg, and Mike Rinck, "Emotion Simulation During Language Comprehension," *Psychonomic Bulletin & Review* 14, no. 3 (2007).

22. David A. Havas et al., "Cosmetic Use of Botulinum Toxin-A Affects Processing of Emotional Language," *Psychological Science* 21, no. 7 (2010).

23. Joshua D. Davis, Piotr Winkielman, and Seana Coulson, "Facial Action and Emotional Language: ERP Evidence That Blocking Facial Feedback Selectively Impairs Sentence Comprehension," *Journal of Cognitive Neuroscience* 27, no. 11 (2015).

24. F. Foroni and Gün R. Semin, "Language That Puts You in Touch with Your Bodily Feelings," *Psychological Science* 20 (2009). Note that the same manipulation did not work when the readers were primed with adjectives, suggesting that adjectives drive less simulation and emotion.

25. Vergallito et al., "Somatic and Visceral Effects of Word Valence, Arousal and Concreteness in a Continuum Lexical Space" (2019).

26. Jeanette Altarriba and Lisa M. Bauer, "The Distinctiveness of Emotion Concepts: A Comparison between Emotion, Abstract, and Concrete Words," *The American Journal of Psychology* 117, no. 3 (2004): 389–410.

27. Berger, Moe, and Schweidel, "What Leads to Longer Reads? Psychological Drivers of Reading Online Content" (2019). As an aside, you might wonder if outside emotion *caused* people to keep reading. Berger's team ran a separate experiment with 300 people. Before asking people to read passages, they primed them by asking them to write about a time when they felt anxiety, anger, or sadness. Then they had people read a couple of paragraphs of an emotionally neutral news story about wireless phones. They requested at the end that people rate their interest in reading more of the news story. When people were primed with anxiety and anger, they *did* want to read more. The reverse was true with sadness. So, the emotional priming before reading had a spillover effect during reading.

28. Al-Rawi, "Viral News on Social Media. "

29. Wansink, Painter, and Ittersum, "Descriptive Menu Labels' Effect on Sales."

30. David A. Havas and Christopher B. Chapp, "Language for Winning Hearts and Minds: Verb Aspect in US Presidential Campaign Speeches for Engaging Emotion," *Frontiers in Psychology* 7 (2016).

31. Daniel Kahneman, *Thinking, Fast and Slow.* (New York: Farrar, Straus, and Giroux, 2011), 140.

32. In Book 2 of *Nicomachean Ethics*, Aristotle says "to have these feelings at the right times on the right grounds towards the right people for the right motive and in the right way is . . . the mark of virtue." As quoted in Maya Tamir et al., "The Secret to Happiness: Feeling Good or Feeling Right?," *Journal of Experimental Psychology: General* 146, no. 10 (2017).

33. Charles Darwin, *On the Origin of Species* (London: John Murray, 1859), https://archive.org/stream/originofspecies00darwuoft/originofspecies 00darwuoft_djvu.txt.

34. "Henry David Thoreau," Lapham's Quarterly, https://www.laphamsquarterly .org/contributors/thoreau.

35. Atul Gawande, *Being Mortal* (New York: Henry Holt, 2014), 79.

36. Jana Lüdtke and Arthur M. Jacobs, "The Emotion Potential of Simple Sentences: Additive or Interactive Effects of Nouns and Adjectives?," *Frontiers in Psychology* 6 (2015). See also Jacobs et al., "10 Years of BAWL-ing into Affective and Aesthetic Processes in Reading: What Are the Echoes?"

37. *Biglari Holdings Annual Report* 2016, http://www.biglariholdings.com /financials/2016/Reports/Biglari%20Holdings%20Annual%20Report %202016.pdf.

38. Daniel Kahneman, *Thinking, Fast and Slow*, 367.

39. David Hauser and Megan Fleming, "Mother Nature's Fury: Antagonist Metaphors for Natural Disasters Increase Forecasts of Their Severity and Encourage Evacuation," *Science Communication* 43, no. 5 (2021).

40. Francesca Citron and others have studied the impact of metaphor on the brain. In the simplest of experiments, Citron found that taste metaphors— "She looked at him sweetly"—turned on simulation and sparked action in the amygdala. The images showed up in fMRIs. See Francesca M. M. Citron and Adele E. Goldberg, "Metaphorical Sentences Are More Emotionally Engaging Than Their Literal Counterparts," *Journal of Cognitive Neuroscience* 26, no. 11 (2014). See also a review of twenty-two MRI studies: Isabel C. Bohrn, Ulrike Altmann, and Arthur M. Jacobs, "Looking at the Brains Behind Figurative Language—A Quantitative Meta-Analysis of Neuroimaging Studies on Metaphor, Idiom, and Irony Processing," *Neuropsychologia* 50, no. 11 (2012).

In another experiment, Citron scanned people who read two- to four-sentence news stories. Some stories used metaphorical phrases, others literal counterparts. Stories featured figurative phrases as simple as "inflation was sinking" versus literal ones like "inflation was lower." She found the stories with figurative words triggered four peaks of action in the readers' amygdala, compared to one for the literal stories. See Francesca M. M. Citron et al., "Conventional Metaphors in Longer Passages Evoke Affective Brain Response," *NeuroImage* 139 (2016).

In yet another study, Citron found that even common idioms (clichés, e.g., "spill the beans") spark some emotional arousal. See Francesca M. M. Citron et al., "When Emotions Are Expressed Figuratively: Psycholinguistic and Affective Norms of 619 Idioms for German (PANIG)," *Behavior Research Methods* 48, no. 1 (2016).

41. Dale Carnegie, *How to Win Friends and Influence People* (New York: Simon & Schuster, 1936), 198.

42. Steve Calandrillo, "5 Ways Life Would Be Better If It Were Always Daylight Savings Time," *The Conversation,* March 3, 2020, https:// theconversation.com/5-ways-life-would-be-better-if-it-were-always -daylight-saving-time-111506.

43. Jonathan Swift, "A Critical Essay upon the Faculties of the Mind," 1707. See also Wikiquote, s.v. "Jonathan Swift," last modified August 22, 2022, 00:13, https://en.wikiquote.org/wiki/Jonathan_Swift.

44. Vinodkumar Prabhakaran, Marek Rei, and Ekaterina Shutova, "How Metaphors Impact Political Discourse: A Large-Scale Topic-Agnostic Study Using Neural Metaphor Detection," https://arxiv.org /abs/2104.03928 (2021).

45. Simon Sinek, *Leaders Eat Last* (New York: Portfolio, 2014), 3.

46. Siddhartha Mukherjee, *The Emperor of All Maladies: A Biography of Cancer* (New York: Scribner, 2010), 1.

47. Andrea Rock, *The Mind at Night* (New York: Basic Books, 2004), 1.

48. Mark Twain, "Corn-Pone Opinions," 1925. For the full text, see https:// americandigest.org/corn-pone-opinions-mark-twain/ or https://www .thoughtco.com/corn-pone-opinions-by-mark-twain-1690231.

Chapter 5: Keep It Seductive

1. Wallace Stegner, *Beyond the Hundredth Meridian: John Wesley Powell and the Second Opening of the West* (New York: Penguin, 1992), 59–60.

2. Jeroen Nawijn et al., "Vacationers Happier, but Most Not Happier after a Holiday," *Applied Research in Quality of Life* 5, no. 1 (2010). See also a follow-up study done with scenarios: Lujun Su, Binli Tang, and Jeroen Nawijn, "Eudaimonic and Hedonic Well-Being Pattern Changes: Intensity and Activity," *Annals of Tourism Research* 84 (2020).

3. Kou Murayama, "A Reward-Learning Framework of Knowledge Acquisition: An Integrated Account of Curiosity, Interest, and Intrinsic–Extrinsic Rewards," *Psychological Review* 129, no. 1 (2022).

4. Marco Magnani, *Creating Economic Growth* (New York: Palgrave Macmillan, 2014), 135.

5. For one early meta-study of the power of anticipation, see Brian Knutson and Stephanie M. Greer, "Anticipatory Affect: Neural Correlates and Consequences for Choice," *Philosophical Transactions of the Royal Society B: Biological Sciences* 363, no. 1511 (2008).

6. George Loewenstein, "Anticipation and the Valuation of Delayed Consumption," *The Economic Journal* 97, no. 387 (1987).

7. Loewenstein, "Anticipation and the Valuation of Delayed Consumption."

8. Kiyohito Iigaya et al., "The Value of What's to Come: Neural Mechanisms Coupling Prediction Error and the Utility of Anticipation," *Science Advances* 6, no. 25 (2020).

9. Kenji Kobayashi and Ming Hsu, "Common Neural Code for Reward and Information Value," *Proceedings of the National Academy of Sciences* 116, no. 26 (2019).

10. Flavia Filimon et al., "The Ventral Striatum Dissociates Information Expectation, Reward Anticipation, and Reward Receipt," *Proceedings of the National Academy of Sciences* 117, no. 26 (2020): 15200–208.

11. Many years of research confirm the flow of dopamine in response to anticipation. As a recent example, see Filimon et al., "The Ventral Striatum Dissociates Information Expectation, Reward Anticipation, and Reward Receipt."

12. For one recent, detailed treatment of the neuroscience, see Lily FitzGibbon, Johnny King L. Lau, and Kou Murayama, "The Seductive Lure of Curiosity: Information as a Motivationally Salient Reward," *Current Opinion in Behavioral Sciences* 35 (2020). See also Elka Stefanova et al., "Anticipatory Feelings: Neural Correlates and Linguistic Markers," *Neuroscience & Biobehavioral Reviews* 113 (2020).

13. Wassiliwizky et al., "The Emotional Power of Poetry: Neural Circuitry, Psychophysiology and Compositional Principles."

14. Zhiwei Li, Neil Bramley, and Todd Gureckis, "Expectations about Future Learning Influence Moment-to-Moment Feelings of Suspense," *Cognition and Emotion* 35, no. 6 (2021).

15. Min Jeong Kang et al., "The Wick in the Candle of Learning: Epistemic Curiosity Activates Reward Circuitry and Enhances Memory," *Psychological Science* 20, no. 8 (2009).

16. Johnny King L. Lau et al., "Shared Striatal Activity in Decisions to Satisfy Curiosity and Hunger at the Risk of Electric Shocks," *Nature Human Behaviour* 4, no. 5 (2020). Note that, in the end, Lau and his team did not administer the shocks. But most readers, later polled, expected they

would. They knowingly took a shock risk just to get a shred of information with no personal benefit.

17. Christopher Hsee, Bowen Ruan, and Zoe Y. Lu, "Creating Happiness by First Inducing and Then Satisfying a Desire: The Case of Curiosity," *ACR North American Advances in Consumer Research* 43 (2015).

18. Rachit Dubey, Tom Griffiths, and Tania Lombrozo, "If It's Important, Then I'm Curious: Increasing Perceived Usefulness Stimulates Curiosity," *Cognition* 226 (2022): 105193.

19. Matthias J. Gruber, Bernard D. Gelman, and Charan Ranganath, "States of Curiosity Modulate Hippocampus-Dependent Learning Via the Dopaminergic Circuit," *Neuron* 84, no. 2 (2014). One other interesting finding by Gruber's team? Although the core part of the reward circuit, the nucleus accumbens, ventral tegmental area, and substantia nigra (page 488) fired heavily during the anticipatory period for curious readers, as shown in fMRI scans, it was quiet when people learned the answer.

20. Wallace Stegner, *Beyond the Hundredth Meridian: John Wesley Powell and the Second Opening of the West* (New York: Penguin, 1992), 66.

21. Robert Sapolsky, *Behave* (New York: Penguin, 2018), 3.

22. Neil Shubin, *Your Inner Fish* (New York: Vintage, 2008), 82.

23. Kahneman, *Thinking, Fast and Slow*, 109.

24. They may not be a good set up for a headline, however. A team lead by Akshina Banerjee at the University of Chicago used natural language processing to examine which headlines in online Upworthy stories prompted the most click-throughs. In other words, which ones made the best "click bait"? They found that headlines with question marks and "interrogative words" *reduced* click-throughs slightly compared to alternatives. See Akshina Banerjee and Oleg Urminsky, "The Language That Drives Engagement: A Systematic Large-Scale Analysis of Headline Experiments." Available at SSRN 3770366 (2021).

25. David Markowitz, "Are People Lying More Since the Rise of Social Media and Smartphones?" *The Conversation,* November 8, 2021, https://theconversation.com/are-people-lying-more-since-the-rise-of-social-media-and-smartphones-170609.

26. Josh Sullivan and Angela Zutavern, *The Mathematical Corporation* (New York: PublicAffairs, 2017), 190.

27. Steven D. Levitt and Stephen J. Dubner, *Freakonomics* (New York: William Morrow, 2005), 19.

28. Jonathan Daniel Leavitt, "Motivations for Reading Stories: Hedonic Responses to Fictionality and Suspense" (Dissertation, University of California, San Diego, 2013).

29. John Krakauer, *Into Thin Air* (New York: Villard [Random House], 1997), 6.

Chapter 6: Keep It Smart

1. A letter from Samuel Johnson, *in* James Boswell, *The Life of Samuel Johnson* (London: Charles Dilly, 1791). See also Wikiquote, s.v. "Samuel Johnson," last modified July 12, 2022, 18:18, https://en.wikiquote.org/wiki /Samuel_Johnson#Elegy_on_the_Death_of_Mr._Robert_Levet,_A _Practiser_in_Physic_(1783).
2. Charlotte Brontë, *Jane Eyre* (London: Smith, Elder, & Co, 1847).
3. James Baldwin, *Notes of a Native Son* (Boston: Beacon Press, 1955).
4. Alex Pine et al., "Knowledge Acquisition Is Governed by Striatal Prediction Errors," *Nature Communications* 9, no. 1 (2018). Key results appear in figure 3. An incidental finding by Pine and his team: The higher people's confidence in their answers, the easier it was to trick them. In a subset of trials, researchers displayed the *wrong* answers after some quiz questions. The readers, thus misled, tested a week later, had by then confidently supplanted the right answers with the wrong ones—more confidently than if they had not been so confident in the first place. You can see how effective propaganda can be: When someone corrects your errors, even when you were sure you were right in the first place, you pay special attention—not always for the better, as you're then doubly sure you're right about the wrong facts.
5. Pablo Ripollés et al., "The Role of Reward in Word Learning and Its Implications for Language Acquisition," *Current Biology* 24, no. 21 (2014).
6. Scientists call this the "compound remote associates task."
7. Martin Tik et al., "Ultra-High-Field fMRI Insights on Insight: Neural Correlates of the Aha!-Moment," *Human Brain Mapping* 39, no. 8 (2018).
8. Yongtaek Oh et al., "An Insight-Related Neural Reward Signal," *NeuroImage* 214 (2020). The initial signal, with insight, came about 500 milliseconds before people pushed the button. About 100 milliseconds later came another surge. Oh and his team did not find any analytical signal whose strength exceeded that of insight ones. The insight signal could reflect just dopamine driving the reward circuit. It could also reflect natural opioids in pleasure hotspots, a source of conscious pleasure.
9. Jasmin M. Kizilirmak et al., "Learning of Novel Semantic Relationships Via Sudden Comprehension Is Associated with a Hippocampus-Independent Network," *Consciousness and Cognition* 69 (2019). See also Jasmin M. Kizilirmak et al., "Neural Correlates of Learning from Induced Insight: A Case for Reward-Based Episodic Encoding," *Frontiers in Psychology* 7 (2016).

10. Margaret E. Webb, Daniel R. Little, and Simon J. Cropper, "Once More with Feeling: Normative Data for the Aha Experience in Insight and Noninsight Problems," *Behavior Research Methods* 50, no. 5 (2018).

11. Author interview with Mark Beeman, professor of psychology at Northwestern University, May 9, 2022.

12. Oh et al., "An Insight-Related Neural Reward Signal."

13. John Kounios and Mark Beeman, "The Cognitive Neuroscience of Insight," *Annual Review of Psychology* 65 (2014).

14. Wangbing Shen et al., "In Search of the 'Aha!' Experience: Elucidating the Emotionality of Insight Problem-Solving," *British Journal of Psychology* 107, no. 2 (2016). See also a recent study of the aha moment as reported across human experience: Øystein O. Skaar and Rolf Reber, "The Phenomenology of Aha-Experiences," *Motivation Science* 6, no. 1 (2020).

15. This is known as transcranial direct current stimulation, or tDCS. Carola Salvi et al., "TDCS to the Right Anterior Temporal Lobe Facilitates Insight Problem-Solving," *Scientific Reports (Nature Publisher Group)* 10, no. 946 (2020).

16. Brooks Atkinson (ed.), *The Essential Writings of Ralph Waldo Emerson* (New York: Modern Library [Random House, 2000], 265.

17. Kounios and Beeman, "The Cognitive Neuroscience of Insight."

18. Widely credited to Virginia Woolf. Original source unknown.

19. Nate Silver, *The Signal and the Noise* (New York: Penguin, 2012), 446.

20. Roger Fisher and William Ury, *Getting to Yes* (New York: Penguin, 1983), 116.

21. Max De Pree, *Leadership Is an Art* (New York: Doubleday, 1987), 11.

22. Irving Stone, *Men to Match My Mountains* (New York: Penguin, 1956), 64.

23. Ronald A. Howard and Clinton Korver, *Ethics for the Real World.* (Boston: Harvard Business Press, 2008), 57.

24. Toni Morrison, Nobel Prize lecture, Stockholm, Sweden, December 7, 1993.

25. As cited in Andrea Bowes and Albert Katz, "Metaphor Creates Intimacy and Temporarily Enhances Theory of Mind," *Memory & Cognition* 43, no. 6 (2015).

26. Serena K. Mon et al., "Conventional Metaphors Elicit Greater Real-Time Engagement Than Literal Paraphrases or Concrete Sentences," *Journal of Memory and Language* 121 (2021).

27. Carl Zimmer, *Life's Edge* (New York: Dutton, 2021) xiv.

28. Thomas Friedman, *The World Is Flat* (New York: Farrar, Straus and Giroux: 2005), 5.

29. John Butman, *Breaking Out* (Boston: Harvard Business Review Press, 2013), 135.

30. Research by a team led by Christine Chesebrough shows that analogies evoke the same aha-like feeling as do other insights. See Christine B. Chesebrough, "Conceptual Change Induced by Analogical Reasoning Sparks 'Aha!' Moments" (Thesis, Drexel University, 2021).

31. Helen Czerski, *Storm in a Teacup* (New York: W. W. Norton, 2017), 14.

Chapter 7: Keep It Social

1. Author interview with David Dodell-Feder, University of Rochester, April 25, 2022.

2. Lewis Thomas, *Lives of a Cell* (New York: Penguin, 1978), 43.

3. E. B. White, *The Elements of Style* (New York: Macmillan, 1979), 67.

4. Chris D. Frith, "The Social Brain?," *Philosophical Transactions of the Royal Society of London. Series B, Biological Sciences* 362, no. 1480 (2007).

5. Junaid Salim Merchant, Diana Alkire, and Elizabeth Redcay, "Neural Similarity between Mentalizing and Live Social Interaction," (2021). See also recent research by a team led by Miriam Weaverdyck at Princeton University. The research showed that "mental states" are represented in the same neuroanatomy in the brain whether prompted by pictures or text. The "representations" are "stable." No matter who you are or what mental state you're having, you've having it in the same part of the brain as everyone else. That's not to say there aren't idiosyncratic differences, but just that, broadly, we're all alike. See Miriam E. Weaverdyck, Mark A. Thornton, and Diana I. Tamir, "The Representational Structure of Mental States Generalizes across Target People and Stimulus Modalities," *NeuroImage* 238 (2021).

6. This chapter highlights research done on traits and intentions, but mind-reading extends equally to emotions. See Micah L. Mumper and Richard J. Gerrig, "The Representation of Emotion Inferences," *Discourse Processes* 58, no. 8 (2021).

7. Sören Krach et al., "The Rewarding Nature of Social Interactions," *Frontiers in Behavioral Neuroscience* 4 (2010).

8. Diana I. Tamir and Brent L. Hughes, "Social Rewards: From Basic Social Building Blocks to Complex Social Behavior," *Perspectives on Psychological Science* 13, no. 6 (2018).

9. For the big picture, see Christina Grimm, Joshua Henk Balsters, and Valerio Zerbi, "Shedding Light on Social Reward Circuitry: (Un)Common Blueprints in Humans and Rodents," *The Neuroscientist* (2020); Shinsuke Suzuki and John P. O'Doherty, "Breaking Human Social Decision Making into Multiple Components and Then Putting Them Together Again," *Cortex* 127 (2020); Andreas Olsson, Ewelina Knapska, and Björn Lindström, "The Neural and Computational Systems of So-

cial Learning," *Nature Reviews Neuroscience* 21, no. 4 (2020); and Ahmad Abu-Akel and Simone Shamay-Tsoory, "Neuroanatomical and Neuro-chemical Bases of Theory of Mind," *Neuropsychologia* 49, no. 11 (2011).

10. Jamil P. Bhanji and Mauricio R. Delgado, "The Social Brain and Reward: Social Information Processing in the Human Striatum," *Wiley Interdisciplinary Reviews. Cognitive Science* 5, no. 1 (2014).

11. For a meta-analysis of work on theory of mind (mind-reading or men-talizing), see Pascal Molenberghs et al., "Understanding the Minds of Others: A Neuroimaging Meta-Analysis," *Neuroscience & Biobehavioral Reviews* 65 (2016).

12. For a definitive anatomy of mentalizing network, highlighting the TPJ and other regions, see Yin Wang et al., "A Large-Scale Structural and Functional Connectome of Social Mentalizing," *NeuroImage* 236 (2021).

13. When you're reading others' emotions, signals pass through the upper part of the reward circuit and get a hearing in an upper part of the pre-frontal cortex. When you're reading thoughts, signals pass through the lower part of the reward circuit and get interpreted in a lower part of the prefrontal cortex. See Abu-Akel and Shamay-Tsoory, "Neuroanatomical and Neurochemical Bases of Theory of Mind."

14. Rebecca Saxe and Nancy Kanwisher, "People Thinking about Think-ing People: The Role of the Temporo-Parietal Junction in 'Theory of Mind,'" *Neuroimage* 19, no. 4 (2003).

15. Gazzaniga, Ivry, and Mangun, *Cognitive Neuroscience: The Biology of the Mind*, 584.

16. A spot in the prefrontal cortex (the ventral medial PFC and the orbito-frontal cortex, or OFC) operates sort of like a currency exchange. For example, see Christian C. Ruff and Ernst Fehr, "The Neurobiology of Rewards and Values in Social Decision Making," *Nature Reviews Neurosci-ence* 15, no. 8 (2014).

17. For early research, see Paul C. Fletcher et al., "Other Minds in the Brain: A Functional Imaging Study of 'Theory of Mind' in Story Comprehen-sion," *Cognition* 57, no. 2 (1995). For a recent overview, see Matthias Schurz et al., "Toward a Hierarchical Model of Social Cognition: A Neuroimaging Meta-Analysis and Integrative Review of Empathy and Theory of Mind," *Psychological Bulletin* 147, no. 3 (2020).

18. Saxe and Kanwisher, "People Thinking about Thinking People: The Role of the Temporo-Parietal Junction in 'Theory of Mind.'" Since the work of Saxe and other researchers, scientists running experiments with false-belief stories have repeatedly replicated the results, confirming the hub role of the TPJ. See David Dodell-Feder et al., "fMRI Item Analysis in a Theory of Mind Task," *Neuroimage* 55, no. 2 (2011): 705–12.

19. Frank Van Overwalle et al., "Spontaneous Goal Inferences Are Often In-ferred Faster Than Spontaneous Trait Inferences," *Journal of Experimental Social Psychology* 48, no. 1 (2012).

20. Frank Van Overwalle and Marie Vandekerckhove, "Implicit and Explicit Social Mentalizing: Dual Processes Driven by a Shared Neural Network," *Frontiers in Human Neuroscience* 7 (2013); and Overwalle et al., "Sponta-neous Goal Inferences Are Often Inferred Faster Than Spontaneous Trait Inferences."

21. Nir Jacoby and Evelina Fedorenko, "Discourse-Level Comprehension Engages Medial Frontal Theory of Mind Brain Regions Even for Ex-pository Texts," *Language, Cognition and Neuroscience* 35, no. 6 (2020).

22. Jorie Koster-Hale and Rebecca Saxe, "Chapter 9: Functional Neuro-imaging of Theory of Mind," in *Understanding Other Minds: Perspectives from Developmental Social Neuroscience*, ed. Simon Baren-Cohen, Helen Tager-Flusberg, and Michael V. Lombardo (Oxford University Press; 3rd edition, 2013).

23. Richard J. Paxton, "The Influence of Author Visibility on High School Students Solving a Historical Problem," *Cognition and Instruction* 20, no. 2 (2002).

24. See three studies: Maria Reichelt et al., "Talk to Me Personally: Person-alization of Language Style in Computer-Based Learning," *Computers in Human Behavior* 35 (2014); Silke Schworm and Klaus D Stiller, "Does Per-sonalization Matter? The Role of Social Cues in Instructional Explana-tions," *Intelligent Decision Technologies* 6, no. 2 (2012); Roxana Moreno and Richard E. Mayer, "Personalized Messages That Promote Science Learning in Virtual Environments," *Journal of Educational Psychology* 96, no. 1 (2004).

25. Richard E. Mayer et al., "A Personalization Effect in Multimedia Learn-ing: Students Learn Better When Words Are in Conversational Style Rather Than Formal Style," *Journal of Educational Psychology* 96, no. 2 (2004): 389–95.

26. Albrecht C. P. Küfner et al., "Tell Me a Story and I Will Tell You Who You Are! Lens Model Analyses of Personality and Creative Writing," *Jour-nal of Research in Personality* 44, no. 4 (2010). A team from Northeastern University came to similar conclusions in a more recent study in which they found a 0.80 correlation between readers' big-five ratings and author personalities. See Judith A. Hall et al., "Individual Differences in Accurately Judging Personality from Text," *Journal of Personality* 84, no. 4 (2016).

27. Mark Miodownik, *Stuff Matters* (New York: Penguin, 2013), ix.

28. Joshua Becker, *Things That Matter* (New York: Waterbrook (Random House), 2022), 3.

29. Hope Jahren, *Lab Girl* (New York: Knopf, 2016), 19.

30. Benjamin K. Bergen, *Louder Than Words* (New York: Basic Books, 2012), 73.

31. Richard A. D'Aveni, *Strategic Capitalism* (New York: McGraw-Hill, 2012), 215.

32. Bowes and Katz, "Metaphor Creates Intimacy and Temporarily Enhances Theory of Mind."

33. Daniel Ariely, *Predictably Irrational* (New York: Harper Collins, 2008), 55.

34. Avinash Dixit and Barry Nalebuff, *The Art of Strategy* (New York: W. W. Norton, 2010), 3.

35. See Benjamin K. Bergen, *Louder Than Words* (New York: Basic Books, 2012), 110. Note that recent research on headlines, using data from A/B testing provided by the website Upworthy, shows that "you" appearing in headlines does *not* increase click-through rates compared to other manipulations. The reason is not clear. This may not relate to a failure to stimulate mind-reading, but instead competition with other "click bait" on the web. See Akshina Banerjee and Oleg Urminsky, "The Language That Drives Engagement: A Systematic Large-Scale Analysis of Headline Experiments," available at SSRN 3770366 (2021).

36. Janine M. Benyus, *Biomimicry* (New York: Harper, 2002) 147–48.

Chapter 8: Keep It Story-Driven

1. Lucas M. Bietti, Ottilie Tilston, and Adrian Bangerter, "Storytelling as Adaptive Collective Sensemaking," *Topics in Cognitive Science* 11, no. 4 (2019).

2. Author interview with Raymond Mar, York University, April 12, 2022.

3. Jeremy Hsu, "The Secrets of Storytelling: Why We Love a Good Yarn," *Scientific American Mind* 19, no. 4 (2008).

4. Michelle Scalise Sugiyama, "Food, Foragers, and Folklore: The Role of Narrative in Human Subsistence," *Evolution and Human Behavior* 22, no. 4 (2001).

5. Yangwen Xu et al., "Brain Network Reconfiguration for Narrative and Argumentative Thought," *Communications Biology* 4, no. 1 (2021).

6. Michael Ventura, *Applied Empathy* (New York: Touchstone, 2018), 7.

7. Bietti, Tilston, and Bangerter, "Storytelling as Adaptive Collective Sensemaking." See also Nick Chater and George Loewenstein, "The Under-Appreciated Drive for Sense-Making," *Journal of Economic Behavior & Organization* 126 (2016).

8. Keith Oatley, "The Mind's Flight Simulator," *The Psychologist* 21, no. 12 (2008), 1030–1032.

9. Sugiyama, "Food, Foragers, and Folklore: The Role of Narrative in Human Subsistence."

10. Aquiles Negrete, "Remembering Rhythm and Rhyme: Memorability of Narratives for Science Communication," *Geoscience Communication* 4, no. 1 (2021).

11. Denis Dutton, "Aesthetics and Evolutionary Psychology," in *The Oxford Handbook for Aesthetics* (New York: Oxford University Press, 2003).

12. Daniel Smith et al., "Cooperation and the Evolution of Hunter-Gatherer Storytelling," *Nature Communications* 8, no. 1 (2017).

13. John K. Donahue and Melanie C. Green, "A Good Story: Men's Storytelling Ability Affects Their Attractiveness and Perceived Status," *Personal Relationships* 23, no. 2 (2016).

14. For more on this subject, see Bietti, Tilston, and Bangerter, "Storytelling as Adaptive Collective Sensemaking."

15. For example, see Mai Nguyen, Tamara Vanderwal, and Uri Hasson, "Shared Understanding of Narratives Is Correlated with Shared Neural Responses," *NeuroImage* 184 (2019); and Jonas T. Kaplan et al., "Processing Narratives Concerning Protected Values: A Cross-Cultural Investigation of Neural Correlates," *Cerebral Cortex* 27, no. 2 (2017).

16. Kaplan et al., "Processing Narratives Concerning Protected Values: A Cross-Cultural Investigation of Neural Correlates."

17. Costa et al., "Emotional Imagery: Assessing Pleasure and Arousal in the Brain's Reward Circuitry." See also Kringelbach and Berridge, "The Affective Core of Emotion: Linking Pleasure, Subjective Well-Being, and Optimal Metastability in the Brain."

18. Jessica Flannery and her team at Florida International University performed a meta-analysis to document the multiple networks in the brain that interact with the reward circuit. See Jessica S. Flannery et al., "Meta-Analytic Clustering Dissociates Brain Activity and Behavior Profiles across Reward Processing Paradigms," *Cognitive, Affective, & Behavioral Neuroscience* 20, no. 2 (2020).

19. Ulrike Altmann et al., "The Power of Emotional Valence—from Cognitive to Affective Processes in Reading," *Frontiers in Human Neuroscience* 6 (2012).

20. Variously the dorsal medial prefrontal cortex, ventral medial prefrontal cortex, and/or orbitofrontal cortex.

21. John McPhee, *Basin and Range* (New York: Farrar, Straus and Giroux, 1982), 165.

22. Your medial frontal cortex.

23. Raymond Mar, then at the University of Toronto, was early in pointing out that many of the same parts of the brain go to work for both writers creating stories and for readers comprehending them. See Raymond A. Mar, "The Neuropsychology of Narrative: Story Comprehension, Story Production and Their Interrelation," *Neuropsychologia* 42, no. 10 (2004).

24. Asieh Zadbood et al., "How We Transmit Memories to Other Brains: Constructing Shared Neural Representations Via Communication," *Cerebral Cortex* 27, no. 10 (2017). See also Deniz et al., "The Representation of Semantic Information across Human Cerebral Cortex During Listening Versus Reading Is Invariant to Stimulus Modality."

25. Kaplan et al., "Processing Narratives Concerning Protected Values: A Cross-Cultural Investigation of Neural Correlates." For research with similar results, see Morteza Dehghani et al., "Decoding the Neural Representation of Story Meanings across Languages," *Human Brain Mapping* 38, no. 12 (2017).

26. Leila Wehbe et al., "Simultaneously Uncovering the Patterns of Brain Regions Involved in Different Story Reading Subprocesses," *PloS ONE* 9, no. 11 (2014).

27. Mikkel Wallentin et al., "Amygdala and Heart Rate Variability Responses from Listening to Emotionally Intense Parts of a Story," *Neuroimage* 58, no. 3 (2011).

28. Diana I. Tamir et al., "Reading Fiction and Reading Minds: The Role of Simulation in the Default Network," *Social Cognitive and Affective Neuroscience* 11, no. 2 (2016).

29. The Moth, "The Moth Presents Jim O'Grady: Pie Man," November 18, 2008, YouTube video, 7:35, https://www.youtube.com/watch?v=3nZzSUDECLo.

30. Erez Simony et al., "Dynamic Reconfiguration of the Default Mode Network During Narrative Comprehension," *Nature Communications* 7, no. 1 (2016).

31. Ye Yuan, Judy Major-Girardin, and Steven Brown, "Storytelling Is Intrinsically Mentalistic: A Functional Magnetic Resonance Imaging Study of Narrative Production across Modalities," *Journal of Cognitive Neuroscience* 30, no. 9 (2018).

32. Nguyen, Vanderwal, and Hasson, "Shared Understanding of Narratives Is Correlated with Shared Neural Responses." See also Yuan, Major-Girardin, and Brown, "Storytelling Is Intrinsically Mentalistic: A Functional Magnetic Resonance Imaging Study of Narrative Production across Modalities."

33. D. Richardson et al., "Engagement in Video and Audio Narratives: Contrasting Self-Report and Physiological Measures," *Scientific Reports* 10 (2018).

34. Berridge, "Evolving Concepts of Emotion and Motivation."

35. Raymond A. Mar et al., "Memory and Comprehension of Narrative Versus Expository Texts: A Meta-Analysis," *Psychonomic Bulletin & Review* (2021).

36. For a more recent experiment showing the power of narrative in healthcare communications, see Kapil Chalil Madathil and Joel

S. Greenstein, "Designing Comprehensible Healthcare Public Reports: An Investigation of the Use of Narratives and Tests of Quality Metrics to Support Healthcare Public Report Sensemaking," *Applied Ergonomics* 95 (2021).

37. Sheila T. Murphy et al., "Narrative Versus Nonnarrative: The Role of Identification, Transportation, and Emotion in Reducing Health Disparities," *Journal of Communication* 63, no. 1 (2013).

38. Kurt Braddock and James Price Dillard, "Meta-Analytic Evidence for the Persuasive Effect of Narratives on Beliefs, Attitudes, Intentions, and Behaviors," *Communication Monographs* 83, no. 4 (2016).

39. Jaime J. Castrellon et al., "Neural Evidence for Narrative-Based Processing of Evidence and Bias in Juror Decision Making," *bioRxiv* (2021).

40. Melissa Lynne Murphy, "Startup Storytelling: An Analysis of Narrative in Rewards and Equity Based Crowdfunding Campaigns" (Dissertation, University of Texas at Austin, 2018). Other researchers have arrived at similar results. Interestingly, Aaron Anglin at the University of Oklahoma Price College of Business found that crowdfunding stories including a second person's perspective could increase the odds of funding success by more than six times. See Aaron Anglin, "Crafting an Effective Story: A Narrative Theory Approach to Entrepreneurial Fundraising in Crowdfunding" (Dissertation, University of Oklahoma, 2017).

41. Samuel G. B. Johnson and David Tuckett, "Narrative Expectations in Financial Forecasting," *Journal of Behavioral Decision Making* (2021).

42. Robert J. Shiller, 2017. "Narrative Economics," *American Economic Review*, 107 (4): 967–1004.

43. Melanie C. Green and Timothy C. Brock, "The Role of Transportation in the Persuasiveness of Public Narratives," *Journal of Personality and Social Psychology* 79, no. 5 (2000).

44. Maj-Britt Isberner et al., "Empowering Stories: Transportation into Narratives with Strong Protagonists Increases Self-Related Control Beliefs," *Discourse Processes* 56, no. 8 (2019).

45. For instance, in one study of students, those who read a story about a "stupid soccer hooligan" performed worse in tests afterward than those who did not read the story. The sense of stupidity, just from the story character's actions, was apparently infectious. See Markus Appel, "A Story About a Stupid Person Can Make You Act Stupid (or Smart): Behavioral Assimilation (and Contrast) as Narrative Impact," *Media Psychology* 14, no. 2 (2011).

46. Franziska Hartung et al., "When Fiction Is Just as Real as Fact: No Differences in Reading Behavior between Stories Believed to Be Based on True or Fictional Events," *Frontiers in Psychology* 8 (2017).

47. Robin Boneck, David Christensen, and Gerald Calvasina, "Whistle While You Work?" *CPA Journal*, April/May 2021.

48. Author interview with Raymond Mar, York University, April 12, 2022.

49. Susan Cain, *Quiet* (New York: Crown, 2013), 19.

50. V. S. Ramachandran, *The Tell-Tale Brain* (New York: W. W. Norton, 2011), 245.

51. Richard A. D'Aveni, *Strategic Capitalism* (New York: McGraw-Hill, 2012), 123.

52. Teddy Roosevelt, 1910, "Citizenship in a Republic," https://theodoreroosevelt.org/content.aspx?page_id=22&club_id=991271&module_id=339364.

53. Upton Sinclair, *The Brass Check: A Study of American Journalism* (Self-published, 1919), chapter 40.

54. Joseph Conrad, *The Mirror of the Sea* (New York: Doubleday, Page, & Company, 1906), chapter XXXV.

55. V. S. Ramachandran, *The Tell-Tale Brain*, 247.

56. Louisa May Alcott, *Hospital Sketches,* 1863.

Afterword: Rewards from Within

1. Victor Hugo, *Les Misérables* (New York: Bigelow, Smith & Company, ca 1862) volume IV (St. Denis), book VII, chapter 1, 184.

INDEX

ABOUT THE AUTHOR

(SUZANNE BIRCHARD)

BILL BIRCHARD has served authors for 25 years as a book consultant, collaborator, and writing coach. His work for other authors includes 15 books of nonfiction on management, health, economics, business, policy, technology, and the environment. Works of his own include *Merchants of Virtue* (Palgrave Macmillan, 2011), *Stairway to Earth* (Birchard Books, 2011), *Nature's Keepers* (Jossey-Bass, 2005), *The One-Minute Meditator* (Da Capo, 2001), and *Counting What Counts* (Basic Books, 2000). Once a magazine editor and later a freelance journalist for *Fast Company*, *CFO*, and *Strategy+Business*, he writes today about the neuroscience and psychology of writing. He lives in Amherst, New Hampshire.

See more at billbirchard.com.